HOW TO ADVERTISE YOUR AUTOMOTIVE RECYCLING YARD

...or any business!

Plus Marketing tips

Mike French

Published by Mike French Publishing

1619 Front Street, Lynden, WA 98264

ISBN: 978-0-9717031-9-3

Printed in the United States of America

This publication is designed to provide accurate and authoritative information with regard to the subject matter covered. It is sold with the understanding that the publisher is not engaged in rendering legal, accounting, or other professional advice. If legal advice or other expert assistance is required, the services of a qualified professional person should be sought.

– From a Declaration of Principles jointly adopted by a Committee of the American Bar Association and a Committee of Publishers and Associations.

This book is dedicated to Roger French, who taught me the importance of hard work, integrity, and honesty. He told me it didn't matter where you worked, because you could work your way to the top in any job if you showed up early, worked hard, left late, and if you did everything you could to make the company you worked for prosper, and he demonstrated it wherever he worked! He was also a faithful husband to my mother and always put her first. I never once heard him complain about anything, even when he was sick. He was truly the best man I have ever known! I miss you dad!

Acknowledgements

I would like to thank: Rachel Vos, for the cover design and photo, Susan French and Laura Williams for editing the articles, and Mark French, for the inside page layout and design.

I would like to thank Dan Kennedy for first introducing me to direct response marketing. What I learned from him changed everything for me about how to get amazing and measurable advertising results.Much of what I talk about in this book, I learned from him.

I would like to thank the late great Zig Ziglar, who taught me to focus on making others successful as my number one goal, the importance of having the right attitude, and to persevere through thick and thin because good things come to those who do.

I'd like to thank my dear friend and fellow publisher, Bette Filley, who taught me early on that success is already in my own hands and that I would do very well if I would consciously look for it, find it, then put it to work. She was so right!

And I would like to thank my longtime friend, Ron Sturgeon, a true marketing genius without a doubt, who has given me much help, encouragement and many valuable insights into marketing to the automotive recycling industry

Contents

Foreword

I was both pleased and honored when Mike French asked me to write the foreword to this book. I first met Mike French in the 1988 when I was busy building and a small single-location salvage yard into the business that I sold to Ford in 1999. Mike and I met while we were networking at an auto salvage convention.

Of course, the way parts were sold in the 1980s was far different. His first work for me was on a project to sell auto parts nationwide, which was unheard of at the time, and subsequently earned me a nice 4-page write up in Inc. Magazine. Mike's later work for me was a direct mail piece that helped to make the All-You-Can-Carry sales days that I used to do a much bigger success. During all the years that I was building my auto salvage business, Mike French gave me crucial insights about how to market to my customers. He has always been innovative and ahead of the curve. He helped me understand who my customers were and how to reach them at the lowest possible cost.

Mike French is still helping me to promote business as diverse as exotic auto rental, self-storage, beauty salons, and business consulting. He even published my first 5 books.

Mike French is also a master of what sometimes seems like a lost art: client service. Even when Mike's quote contains a mistake in the client's favor, Mike honors the quote as given. Not every businessperson has the integrity or long-term orientation to do that.

Mike French does.

One the rare occasion that any promotional material he has created has a substantial error, Mike reprints at his expense.

He is always the person that I recommend to business owners seeking help doing promotions of any kind and he has been for decades. If you are engaged in building a salvage business, or any other kind of business, Mike French & Company is an extraordinarily valuable resource.

Through the years, as the publisher of Auto Recycler's Toolbox, Mike has always been willing to share business-building ideas with auto recyclers.

His ideas, the ideas in this book, have helped me to be much more successful. Read, study, and apply them. My wish is that they do the same for you.

Ron Sturgeon

Introduction

This book is a compilation of published articles I've written over my career of specializing in advertising services and products for the Automotive Recycling Industry.

The direct response methods and principles I've explained throughout this book are tried and proven transferable marketing concepts which will work very well when applied to any type of business that involves selling products and/or services to people, whether it's a salvage yard selling auto parts, a realtor selling properties, an artist selling art, or even a flower shop selling floral arrangements. No matter what type of advertising concept or method you choose to use to promote your business, products or service you will succeed or fail based on your ability to work successfully and persuasively with people. I agree wholeheartedly with what the former Coca Cola Company CEO, Robert Woodruff, said in the little handout pamphlet he created, which I quote here from Zig Ziglar's book, "Top Performance" 1, where he said:

> *"Life is pretty much a selling job. Whether you succeed or fail is largely a matter of how well we motivate the human beings with whom we deal to buy us and what we have to offer.*
>
> *Success or failure in this job is essentially a matter of human relationships. It is a matter of the kind of reaction to us by our family members, customers, employees, employers, and*

fellow workers and associates. If this reaction is favorable we are quite likely to succeed. If the reaction is unfavorable we are doomed.

The deadly sin in our relationship with people is that we take them for granted. We do not make an active or continuous effort to do and say things that will make them like us, and believe us, and that will create in them the desire to work with us in the attainment of our desires and purposes.

Again and again, we see both individuals and organizations perform only to a small degree of their potential success, or fail entirely, simply because of their neglect of the human element in business and life.

They take people and their actions for granted. Yet it is these people and their responses, that make or break them."

Zig Ziglar, Top Performance: How to Develop Excellence in Yourself and Orhers (New York: Berkley Publishing Group)

The following articles were written by me over many years for a number of different automotive recycler publications, so there is undoubtedly some duplication here and there of important marketing principles, methods or strategies. I hope any duplication will help you remember them.

Chapter 1
How to get your advertising offer chosen first

When I was a kid, my school had a simple method for creating teams for games. Two captains took turns selecting team members - one at a time, back and forth, until every kid was chosen to be on a team. Kids waiting to be chosen jumped up and down, waving their arms and yelling, "Choose me! Choose me!"

I hated this! I was always the last kid chosen. Even then, neither side wanted me on their team. It was probably because I was smaller than all the other kids. I also had vision problems and couldn't see the ball very well, handicapping any team that was forced to have me. It was humiliating!

As the years went by, I worked hard to not be the last kid chosen for a team. I practiced playing better and got glasses to help me see the ball. And I grew bigger. Eventually it paid off and I wasn't the last kid chosen anymore. Although this was an improvement, I really wanted to be the FIRST kid chosen!

Choose-me-first attitude

When I got into the advertisement business, I brought this "choose-me-first" attitude with me. I wanted the advertising I created for companies to work better than anyone else's. I did research to find out what made consumers choose to buy products and services from one company over another and what made one advertisement stand out above the rest.

I discovered two things

DESCRIBE VERY WELL

How well something is described determines an ad's success way ahead of the cost.

I did a lot of research for answers. I thought cost or money would be the biggest deciding factor in buying decisions but that wasn't it! It was other things, such as the item's popularity, its availability in the marketplace, how attractive it was in the ad, or how well it was described that determined success way ahead of the cost. If the consumer was persuaded by the ad copy and illustrations, price didn't matter! That explains why so many Americans have so much debt for buying things like fancy cars, expensive smart phones and big TVs. They want the items based on the ads, no matter the cost.

Sometimes consumers will make buying decisions for ridiculous reasons when they are not given a solid reason to respond to an advertisement. By ridiculous reasons I mean, they may buy one item over another because it costs one penny less. The product was $9.99 in once place and $10.00 in another ad on the same page. The one for $9.99 won because it was not about the penny, but about making a buying decision, and one cent was the deciding factor for the choice.

Many ads look alike

Auto recycler ads, especially in groupings like in magazines or The Yellow Pages, tend to look alike so consumers can't decide who to call. I have written about this many times in the past, but the problem still persists. Most recycler ads have the name of their company, such as "XYZ's Auto Parts" at the top. They may have a picture of an engine or transmission, their address, phone number, and logo. That's it! There are no selling headlines or offers to respond to. There is no call to action, no reason to call. When someone looks at the page of ads, they don't know who to call based on this information. This is unfortunate because when someone goes to the yellow pages, they are ready to buy and don't know who to buy from.

Buyers need clear reasons to respond

How can you get people to respond to your advertisement first? The answer is really simple. Give them clear reasons why they must respond to you first. The more reasons you give them, the more powerful your ad will be! Each reason should clearly answer the customer's biggest question, which is, "What's in it for me?" List as many reasons as you can and tell them boldly to call you first! Say something like: "These are the reasons you should call us first!"

WHAT'S IN IT FOR ME?

Give solid reasons for consumers to respond to your advertisement. Each reason should answer their biggest question, "What's in it for me?"

To get your creative juices flowing, here are some things you can include in your ads to get people to respond to you first.

Show that you are EASY to do business with!

Convenience trumps price when it comes to what consumers value. Here are some ideas: You are easy to find. It's easy to buy from you. It's easy to pay. You are open longer hours. It's easy to find parking. It's easy to get repairs, updates, and modifications. It's easy to get delivery or installation. It's easy to get related parts, supplies, and answers. It's easy to get expert advice or assistance. It's easy to find products and to select what you want.

Show clearly what you provide.

List clearly the products and services you provide. List the benefits of doing business with you. Here are some ideas: You provide free parking. You provide free pick up or delivery within a certain area and time frame. You provide multiple ways to deliver. You have a secure, guarded location. You accept competitors' coupons. You are open 24-hours a day. You are open weekends. You have a round-the-clock mechanic on site. You have express check-in or check-out. You have a frequent buyer program. You make walk-ins welcome. You give free demonstrations. You offer free on site assistance and free technical support. You offer a list of convenient locations. You offer a free newsletter and easy online

A GOOD HEADLINE TO USE

"Here are reasons to call me first!"

WHAT CONSUMERS VALUE MOST

Convenience trumps price when it comes to what a consumer values most so list as many as you can in your advertising.

24/7 shopping. Your staff is trained and/or certified and list what kind it is.

Identify yourself to those who require extra attention or have special requirements:

You have a smoke free environment. You have someone on staff to pull all your items for you. You have elevator access. You have sign language available. You have staff who speak the following languages (list them). Your facilities are wheelchair accessible. Pets are welcome. You have senior discounts. You have rides available upon request. You have motorized scooters available.

List CAUSES you support or care about.

Your products are made in your country. You give a percentage of every sale to (list cause). You collect for charity with all proceeds for (list charity); you support the local high school band (or other cause).

There you have it! Now you can put together an ad that will get people to respond to you first!

Chapter 2
How to get the "slight-edge-advantage" in your advertising projects

It is amazing how close some Olympic participants are at the finish line, some win by a photo finish. The difference between winners and losers is often infinitesimal, maybe a slight fraction of a second; yet the top prize, along with all the glory and its benefits go only to the winner. The winner gets 100% of the top prize. Does this mean the winner was 100% better than the losing competitor? No. What it means is the winner had the winning edge and that winning edge made all the difference in the world.

The same can be said about advertising in today's marketplace. Obtaining even the slightest edge over your competitor does make the difference in whether or not you make a sale. You don't usually have to be a whole lot better than your competitor to get the sale; you only need to be slightly better than them. This is also true in landing job bids.

I recently listened to an interview with a star salesman who had consistently been

GET THE
WINNING
EDGE

You don't usually have to be a whole lot better than your competitor to get the sale; you only need to be slightly better than them.

the top producer in every sales venture he had been involved in. The list of where he had worked was long and impressive yet he always topped every other salesperson no matter which company he was involved in or what product he was selling.

The interviewer asked him to reveal his big secret in selling. "It's nothing amazing, really." He said. "All I did was to return every prospect's call immediately upon receiving it. This gave me the edge over everyone else who puts follow-up off until later." For him, this "edge" worked because most people who enquire about a product or service are in fact ready to buy when they call. By following up immediately, he usually got the sale. By the way, most people who enquire about a product or service eventually do purchase that product or service, but not necessarily from the first salesperson they spoke with! Salespeople who put off following up until a later time usually lose the sale to someone else.

FOLLOW-UP FAST

ALWAYS do follow-up immediately; it will pay off more than you think!

The "good-old-days" in marketing

The first direct mail project I did for an auto recycler way back in the 1980's was easy and uncomplicated. I just took some black and white photos of wrecked cars, lined them up in rows on each page, printed the job on cheap newsprint and mailed it to a large list of auto repair shops. Soon the phones started to ring off the hook. They had no trouble knowing when the mailing had been delivered by the post office because the response was fast and dramatic. In fact, the phones were already ringing when the counter staff arrived for work. They took one call after another without letup. As soon as they put the phone receiver down, the phone rang again with a new order. The staff had never worked so hard! The phones were still ringing at the end of the day when they left. The phones stayed jammed for days.

That was then, and this is now!

In today's marketplace, it is nearly impossible to get a landslide response to any kind of advertising campaign or promotion. Why is this? To begin with, back when we sent out our first mailer, hardly any salvage yard was doing professional advertising. Many are now, and as a result, today's marketplace is very different. Consumers now face an avalanche of advertisements coming at them from every direction. It arrives by mail, regular telephone & smartphone, email, faxes, all kinds of social media and the Internet. Then there is advertising aimed at them on television and radio. They also see it on signs along the road, on buildings and the side of vehicles of all kinds. It is printed on clothing and thousands of promotional products. It's even in some previously unthinkable places. I read in this morning's newspaper that you will soon be able to buy advertising on postage stamps. It's no wonder consumers are becoming blind to advertising.

You now must work harder AND

smarter

Advertisers must work harder and smarter than ever before to get advertising noticed and responded to. You can't "just get your name out there" and expect measurable results. You must study advertising carefully, know what you're doing, and know what causes people to respond. You must create advertising purposefully. It must be intelligently designed to include the right response devices and triggers. Only then will you achieve an "edge" over the competitors marketing in your territory. And yes, don't kid yourself about it, there ARE competitors marketing in YOUR territory. There are large companies like yours, selling the same things you are, advertising and shipping nationwide. A repair shop just down the street from you may receive advertisements from a faraway auto parts provider selling the same parts as you. They may offer attractive coupons and other incentives to make your customers choose them over you. Usually, there is no return address on their advertisement to say where they are located. There is only a toll-free number to call to place an order. You can be sure they are getting a response or they wouldn't continue to advertise in your area.

So, what should you do?

First, make sure you are advertising regularly in your own marketplace. Failing to do so will make your customers sitting

ADVERTISE REGULARLY

Make sure you advertise regularly in your own marketplace so your regular customers don't forget about you.

28

ducks for anyone else who is advertising to them.

Secondly, make sure you include the right marketing ingredients in your advertising product mix. Remember the secrets of what makes consumers respond. For example, two ads might appear side by side in the same publication, or arrive together in the same batch of mail. Both are the same size and both cost the same amount of money. The only difference between the two is that one is "benefit" driven and the other is not. Ads that spotlight benefits always edge out ones that don't. But that's only part of it. Good ads must have powerful headlines and subheads, irresistible offers, attention-getting teasers, well-written testimonials, powerful illustrations and photos, valuable coupons, easy-to-understand response devices, correct color choices, strong and professional graphic design, contact information placed in the correct location as well as clear, strong, call-to-action statements.

ALWAYS SPOTLIGHT THE BENEFITS

Ads that spotlight benefits always edge out ones that don't.

By the way, I recently noticed two similar display ads that just happened to be side by side in the daily newspaper for the very same product. Both ads looked exactly alike in size and shape, only one had the price slightly better than the other. One offered it for $30.00 and the other for $29.99—a one cent difference! Guess which one got the calls? You know it wasn't about the penny; it was about having to choose

**BECOME
A DIRECT
MARKETING
STUDENT**

To have that edge,
you must either
become a student
of direct-response
advertising methods
and strategies
yourself or hire a
professional with a
solid track record
to do it for you.

who to buy from when everything looked the same. That buying choice is often made for very small reasons. Very small changes can make a huge difference in response. There was another ad this morning in the newspaper that offered a product, "Two for the price of one." A competitor's ad nearby offered the same product, but said it this way, "Buy one and get one FREE." Both were the same exact offer, but the second one was a better sounding offer. Anyone reading the paper and in the market for that particular product probably saw both ads near each other and had to choose which one to buy. Studies have shown that the second way of wording brings a much better response because it uses the word "free."

So, in today's marketplace, you must know how to get the "slight edge advantage" over competitors rather than expect a landslide by simply "getting your name out there." To have that edge, you must either become a student of direct-response advertising methods and strategies yourself or hire a professional with a solid track record to do it for you. Be careful, though; most graphic designers don't know anything about marketing. They only know how to make pretty flyers and that isn't enough by itself to give you the "marketing edge". Only applied, tried, and proven marketing methods and strategies will give you the winning edge you need!

So, if you want to get the edge over

competitors in advertising, work at making your ads a little better than your competitor's ads in as many areas as you can.

Here are a few ideas

- **Ad Size** - Make your ad a little larger than your competitor's ad to make yours stand out above theirs.

- **Product Offer** - Make sure you have an offer on your advertisement. My rule is, "if there is no offer, then there will be no response", so make sure you have at least one offer in place (more than one is better). By the way, most recycler ads I see include no product offers at all, they just show their logo and business name on their ad; so having any offer on yours is an improvement over theirs.

- **Layout** - Many recycler ads look amateurish and unprofessional. This is especially so because so many use online programs to design their own ads. Make sure your layout includes a great design, looks professional, and draws attention.

- **Graphic Elements** - Use starbursts, call outs, underlining of key words, colored high lighting, arrows, and emblems to draw the eye to the various selling parts of your ad.

- **Secondary Offers** - Use secondary offers to sweeten your deal by saying, "But wait, there's more!" And then include some add-ons such as special

MAKE YOUR ADS A LITTLE BETTER

Because consumers make buying decisions for the smallest of reasons, work at making your ads a little better than your competitors in as many ways as possible.

savings if they order today or a promotional product with their purchase.

- **Provocative headlines** - Most recycler ads do not include headlines; they use the name of their company as a headline, so having any headline at all will be a big improvement. Use bold headlines to highlight as many benefits as you can.

- **Ink Colors** - If your competitor's ads are black and white, use some color on yours. Use a color, such as red, to highlight important things you want buyers to notice within your ad layout.

- **Placement Position** - Place your ad at the top of the page if there are several ads on a page. If your ad is in a magazine, ask to be on the right side page.

- **Photos** - Use product and employee photos. Make sure all your employees are looking right into the camera and smiling.

- **Something Free** - List as many FREE items as you can, such as free local delivery and free product research (if we don't have it, we'll find it for you).

- **Product Price** - Make your prices a little better than theirs. If they sell an item for $50, sell yours for $49.99.

- **Frequency** - Place your ad more often than they do. If they advertise once a month, then do yours every three weeks.

- **Testimonials** - Use satisfied customer testimonials with smiling photos telling why they love your products and services.

- **Coupons** - Use coupons to add value. If your competitors use coupons, make yours better than theirs -- if they give $25 off of a transmission purchase, you give $30. Accept competitor coupons plus perhaps an extra 5-10% off.

There are lots of things you can do to make your advertising slightly better than your competitor's. Always work to make as many small improvements as you can. Those improvements will pay off!

Chapter 3
Lead Generation Marketing

In my opinion, the hardest and worst kind of advertising is cold calling. It will wear you out faster than anything. Many businesses do a lot of cold calling to generate their leads, and it's like trying to dig earthworms through concrete. The cold calling advertising method is nowhere to be found in my arsenal of recommended advertising strategies because there are far better, easier, and even fun ways to get good leads. The first and main reason "cold calling" fails is because you are interrupting and bothering people with a sales call. Nobody likes to receive that kind of call. Second, cold calling fails because you have to dig through a lot of ocean water to locate the right kind of fish. Simply put, most people are not interested in your products and services, and it takes a lot of calls to a lot of uninterested prospects before you just happen upon one that is interested. Then, you may spend a lot of time talking to him, calling him back five or six times, and then you still may not make a sale. No wonder there is such a high burnout rate among businesses that do this.

GET PROSPECTS TO CALL YOU

Use lead generation advertising methods to get prospects to call you!

Will all those interested please raise your hands?

There is much better way to get good quality leads and an easier way to turn them into buying customers. Instead of calling them, you get them to call you! Isn't that a lot easier? You bet it is! It is a lot easier to talk to someone who calls you about your products and services than it is to call them and try to stir up some interest. How do you do this? You advertise for them! You qualify them with your ad so that only the right prospects will call you. This is done through multi-step lead generation advertising.

QUALIFY
PROSPECTS

Qualify prospects with your ad so that only the right prospects will call you.

The idea behind this method of advertising is you aren't trying to make a big sale through the first contact. You are only trying to get good qualified leads to raise their hands, reveal themselves to you, and ask you for information.

Let's say you are at a big convention. The room is filled with thousands of people and you know that your perfect prospects are somewhere in that room. Then someone hands you a microphone and allows you to make an announcement to everybody. You introduce yourself and tell them about your exciting offer. You close by saying, "only those of you who want more information about this exciting offer please raise your hands." When they reveal themselves to you, you give them more information, such as your sales letter, etc.

Who could you reach with this approach? Anyone! You can use this method to reach any kind of prospect such as insurance adjusters, certain kinds of shop owners, whoever. The key is to place advertising in the places your prospects will most likely look such as trade magazines, specific niche market mailing list, and tradeshow publications, just to name a few. Lead generation ads are always a part of multi-step process. They respond to your ad to receive more information, that's step one. You follow up by sending them your direct response package, that's step two. They respond to the information with their order - step three; or they request more information - step four, and so on. You create as many steps as you need to get the final results you want. The amount of steps you use vary, depending on the type and size of your offer. Usually, the bigger the offer, the more steps will be necessary.

Lead Generation Methods

Classified ads/small space ads. This is a fast and very inexpensive way to generate leads. It's also a good way to test headlines, offers, prices, etc.

Free recorded message. Your ad invites them to hear a free recorded message. Your recorded message gives them exciting details and invites them to leave their name, address, and phone number.

Free consumer reports. The ad invites them to ask you for a free consumer

ADVERTISE IN THE RIGHT PLACES

Place your advertising in the most likely places your prospects will look!

BIGGER OFFERS REQUIRE MORE STEPS

The bigger the offer, the more lead generation steps are necessary. Make sure you create as many as you need.

report. The report covers the subject and offers your product as the solution. You can write consumer reports on many hot topics around the interests and concerns of your prospects. For instance, you might write one entitled, "Warning! Six things you must know before buying used vehicle parts!– Call for a free consumer report", and then put your phone number as the contact.

So there you have it! Stop burning yourself out with frustrating and ineffective cold calling and begin turning your prospects into buying customers through lead generation marketing

Chapter 4

Make advertising easy by developing your USP

While attending a business lunch recently, I placed my business card into a basket for a door prize drawing. Later I received a pleasant surprise when the MC pulled my name from the basket and gave me a nice gift. Then he said, "Mike, what does your company do?"

I could have said, "I own an advertising agency," or "I do printing and direct mail," or even, "I provide imprinted promotional products for the recycling industry." All these things I do but I didn't say any of that. Instead, I simply stated my USP. I said, "My Company gets you more customers like your best customers, and we make your phones ring, guaranteed!"

Before I could get out the door, several business owners handed me their business cards and asked me to call them. They wanted me to do for them what I had just said when I repeated my USP.

This shows the power of having a good USP and what it can do for you! It makes advertising easy. It makes sales! Every business needs one!

ANSWER A "WHAT DO YOU DO" QUESTION WITH YOUR USP

When someone asks what you do, tell them your USP, and if they answer, "Really, how do you do that?" then you know you have the right one.

*A USP MUST
ANSWER THIS
IMPORTANT
QUESTIOIN*

"Why should I do
business with you
above all other
options, including
doing nothing,
or whatever I'm
doing right now?"

So what exactly is a USP? Simply put, USP stands for Unique Selling Proposition. It was originally developed by the author of "Reality in Advertising," Rosser Reeves, who said that a company must develop a USP in order to stand out in the crowded marketplace. He said a company does this by clearly communicating the one definable point about itself or its product and service that will capture the attention and stir the emotions of the company's prospective clients. Some of the well-known USPs Reeves created are:

- "Wonder Bread helps build strong bodies twelve ways."

- "M&M's melt in your mouth, not in your hands."

- "Colgate cleans your breath while it cleans your teeth."

According to Dan Kennedy, author of "No B.S. Sales Success," a USP must answer the question for a potential customer: "Why should I do business with you above all other options, including doing nothing, or whatever I'm doing right now?" Kennedy said, "A USP must be specific, concise and meaningful. People should be able to understand it and 'get it' immediately. It must differentiate you from your competitors. It must state at least one unique benefit your customer will receive."

How do you know if you have the correct USP for your company? Kennedy said there is a simple test---when you tell someone your USP, you should get the following response: "Really? How do you do that?" Then you tell them how your products and services accomplish what you said. For example, let's say you're at a party and someone asks you what you do. Instead of saying something ordinary like, "I own a salvage yard," you tell them your USP. You can say, "My Company saves you cash by saving the planet!" There is a good chance the prospect will answer with, "Really, how do you do that?" Then you can tell them how using your recycled parts saves environmental resources while at the same time saving 40% to 60% off the cost of buying new parts.

1. To develop your own USP, answer these two questions:

    •   Other businesses like mine do the following:

        _____.

    •   What I do better than they do:

        _____.

2. Make a list of your biggest customer benefits. Clearly describe how your products or services best answer the customer's question, "What's in it for me?" Think in terms of what your products or services do for your customer and the end result they desire from a product or service like yours. Include the top benefit in your USP. A good example of this is FedEx's USP, "When It Absolutely, Positively Has To Be There Overnight!"

SOLVE A CUSTOMER PAIN PROBLEM

Discover a customer pain problem and solve it with your USP. Colgate toothpaste's USP is a good example: "Colgate cleans your breath while it cleans your teeth."

MAKE YOUR USP SHORT

Short USP's are better than long ones because they are easier for customers to remember. M&M is a great example: "M&M's melt in your mouth, not in your hands."

3. What sets you apart from your competitors? What area of your business do you and your existing customers see you as a leader in? Why are you uniquely different from others doing the same thing as you? Is there something special, unusual, or significant about the way you do business? A good example of this is Bounty Paper Towels, who offer a very absorbent paper towel that soaks up water fast. They created a USP around this feature: "Bounty: The Quicker Picker-Upper."

4. Solve a Pain Problem for your customer or fill a missing gap in your industry. What are the frustrating "pain" problems that your customer experiences in your industry? Stop that pain in your USP. In the pizza industry, it was how long it took to get pizza delivered to the customer's door after they ordered it. It usually took an hour, and it usually came cold! Domino's Pizza solved the problem with their USP: "Hot pizza delivered to your door in 30 minutes or less, or it's free."

5. Your USP should have promises or guarantees to grab attention and compel people to respond. Make sure you can and do deliver on what your USP claims! When FedEx said in their USP that they would absolutely get it to you overnight, they knew they could deliver. They had developed a system that made it possible for them to deliver on their promise consistently.

6. Be concise, specific, and meaningful. Short USP's are better than long ones because they are easier for the customer to remember and they are easier to incorporate into all forms of advertising. The best USP is instantly understood and is meaningful to the consumer. Burger King's USP, "Have it your Way",

quickly gets across the idea to the customer. It says that it's easy for the customer to request changes and get a hamburger prepared exactly the way they like it.

7. Take all the details about your product or service and condense them into one sentence that is clear and concise. Most powerful USPs are written so well that every word is perfectly placed so you cannot change a single one. Every word must work to earn you money by selling your product or service.

Once you have your USP developed, you can include it in all your advertising projects. Use it in everything you print. Use it in sales copy headlines. Use it on your brochures, your signs, and your business cards. Use it on your letterhead, your website, and your telephone "on hold" messages. And, if you do marketing at trade shows, make sure it is prominently seen in your booth display.

Your USP should be the driving force behind all your marketing. Work hard at getting it right and it will work hard for you!

YOUR USP MUST EARN YOU MONEY

Every word in your USP must work to earn you money by selling your product or service.

Chapter 5
How to makes sales in hard economic times like these

Business owners tell me all the time that they aren't getting their advertising done because they are wearing too many hats these days and are distracted by other important things they need to do. But those who advertise are the ones who end up with the lion's share of the business - even during hard economic times. Consumers still need things and will buy them, even in a down economy. Consumers will especially purchase value-priced replacement auto parts. It is even possible to prosper and even outsell the competition in times like these. Here are some suggestions to help you do just that.

Do the Most Important Things First

Even in advertising, you have to schedule important activities in or they won't get done. Charlie "Tremendous" Jones, in his book, "Life is Tremendous", tells the story of a frustrated businessman who asked him for a solution to his problem of never getting important things done. Charlie asked the man to describe a typical business day. After the businessman fin-

DO THE MOST IMPORTANT THINGS FIRST

Even in advertising, you must schedule important activities in or they won't get done. The key to success is to priotise them and do the critical things first until completrd.

45

ished describing his day, Charlie wrote down a simple solution to the problem and handed it to the man. Here's what it said: "Every night before you go to bed, make a list of what you need to accomplish the next day. Then number the list with the most important item being number one, and the second most important thing being number two, and so on. The next day when you get to work, only concentrate on doing the number one item on your list and don't do anything else until it's done. Shut out all distractions. When the first item on your list is completed, cross if off and concentrate on doing the second item. Do as many things as you can from your list for that day in their order of importance. Then, at the end of the day, make an itemized list for the next day and repeat this each following day. You may not get everything on your list done for that day, but you will always get the most important things done. The man took the note, put it in his pocket, and asked Charlie to send him a bill. But Charlie said, "No! Just try my idea for a month, and then send me a check for how much you think its worth." A month later, Charlie received a check in the mail from the man for $10,000! This was during the 1950's when that was a whopping amount of money.

Add value to your products and services
It will make advertising much easier for you! When I first started in the advertising business many years ago, I

proudly showed a friend of mine the ad I had put together to advertise my business. My friend was a very successful salesman whose opinion I greatly respected. He looked at my ad copy which said among other things, "The best prices on the planet!" He frowned and handed me back the ad. He said, "Mike, don't use the sentence about your prices being the best on the planet. If you live by price, you will die by price! So don't go that route in your advertising!" I argued with him, "But, I DO have the best prices in the industry I'm marketing in and I can prove it." He said, "That may be true, Mike, but there will always be someone somewhere who is willing to do it cheaper, and you will always be fighting an uphill battle about price. Instead, you should say something like, 'The best **VALUE** on the planet!' People can always argue price with you, but they can't argue value. Value is made up of things that are hard to measure." He then told me that when people value something, money is no object. For instance, many poor people have big TV sets in their homes because that's what they value and people will ALWAYS find a way to get anything they truly value!

STRESS
VALUE
INSTEAD
OF PRICE

If you live by price you will die by price so always emphasize the value instead of the price!

In other words, you can't always control the price of your products; but that shouldn't stop you from adding more value. Most buying decisions are not based solely on price but on many other factors. People consider ease of purchase, an existing relationship with someone in sales, and the speed of shipping (how fast they will get it). These are things you can work to emphasize and improve.

Improve yourself and how you treat your customers

Dale Carnegie, the author of "How to win friends and influence people," said, "People who are unable to motivate themselves must be content with mediocrity." You have no control over what your competition is doing, so don't worry about that. Instead, concentrate on giving your customers a very positive experience when they buy from you. Work on having a positive attitude - even with difficult customers; smile when you speak to them on the phone and they will hear it. Go the extra mile in getting them what they need. Follow up each sale with a note or phone call to make sure they got what they needed from you.

Never complain

The world is full of complainers. Admittedly, there ARE lots of things in the world to be negative about but don't get caught up in negativity. It will rob you of energy and will spill over onto others. This negativity will affect your ability to sell. Instead, when bad things happen, step back, take a deep breath and ask yourself, "What can I do differently to make something good come out of this? How can I change or take control of this situation instead of complaining about it? Is this something over which I can take control?" And also, "How can I change and improve my sales performance?"

Focus on helping others succeed. I left the most important thing for last. The late, great motivational speaker, Zig Ziglar said, "If you want to be successful in life, work hard to make others successful. By doing so, you will automatically become successful!" He was right. Above all, the number one success principle is to give people and their needs the first priority. Make them as happy and as successful as you possibly can - and in every way that you can. It will come back to you in many ways. You will have repeat customer business as well as their referrals, you will sleep well at night, and you will have a happy life!

MAKE IT ABOUT OTHERS!

If you want to be successful in life, work hard to make others successful. By doing so, you will automatically become successful!"

Chapter 6
Stop spinning your wheels! Grow with goals and a marketing plan!

Most recyclers fail to promote their business properly because they have no defined goals or marketing plans in place. Typically, they get up each morning, go to work, buy a few cars, sell some parts, put out a few fires, go home, and repeat the routine the next day. Time goes by, another year passes and they haven't gotten ahead in business; they've only been spinning their wheels. If they've done any advertising, it was usually a yellow page ad in the phone book. How do I know this? It's because I speak to recyclers daily on the phone, and talk at conferences. I ask them about their marketing plan and this is what they tell me.

Someone has rightfully said, "If you continue to do what you've always done, you'll continue to have what you've always had." The truth is you can't continue to do the same thing, day in and day out, with no goals or marketing plan in place, and expect different results from what you've been getting. You've got to do something

DO SOMETHING DIFFERENT

If you continue to do what you've always done, you will continue to have what you've always had! You've got to do something different! Nothing changes until something changes!

different! Nothing changes until something changes!

If you notice others succeeding in the same business as you and you are spinning your wheels, it is probably because they have a marketing plan in place and are working the plan. If you want to succeed, you need a marketing plan, too; and it starts with a description of what you want to accomplish when promoting your company. It continues with ideas of how you are going to accomplish it. In other words, not having defined goals or a marketing plan is like trying to build a house without a foundation.

HAVE A MARKETING PLAN

It starts with a description of what you want to accomplish when promoting your company. It continues with ideas of how you are going to accomplish it.

There's a Bible story about a foolish man who built his house on the sand. He did it because it was easy digging. Everything was fine until the storm came. According to the story, the rains fell and the winds blew until his house was gone! If you've been in business a while, you can remember when you didn't have to do much marketing to sell parts because there was little competition, business just came along. It was easy digging. But then the storms of competition came! Now customers are being exposed to many buying choices. They receive attractive parts offers from many directions. They get them in the mail, by broadcast fax, by email, and by searching the Internet. They can get parts the next day from all across the country! It is now very common for a salvage yard to ship parts anywhere in the world. Salvage yards on the other side of the country are now your competitors!

These "storms" are causing many salvage yards to change the way they do business. And you must, too! You have to build your business on a hard rock foundation of clearly defined goals with a solid marketing plan to achieve them!

Here's what to do.

Clarify what you want to achieve. Decide where you want to go and what you want to accomplish by defining the target of your marketing plan. Not having a clear, well-defined target is like shooting an arrow into the air and hoping it hits something. Unfortunately, most recyclers just shoot an occasional marketing "arrow" into the air and, predictably, don't hit anything! It's like archery without targets or playing hoopless basketball. Can you imagine what that would be like? Where would you aim? How would you keep score? You need to be able to measure results. You need a way to correct strategies to improve. As outlandish as targetless archery and hoopless basketball may sound to you, that is how many business owners approach their marketing. Without written plans or goals, the results are erratic and difficult to measure.

Do a personal business survey. It's only after you know what the numbers are that you can set goals to increase them. You need to know how many clients you have

DO A PERSONAL BUSINESS SURVEY

It's only after you know what the numbers are that you can set goals to increase them.

per month. You need to know how many are current customers and new customers. You should know how much money you make from each customer and how much it costs you to acquire a new customer.

Consider the big picture

Where do you want your business to be in a few years? Projecting your goals for five years ahead is no longer good enough! How much money do you expect your company to gross and how many employees and customers do you expect your company to have in the next few years? What new equipment and changes in your facility do you need? What steps do you need to take to accomplish each goal? Write each goal at the top of a page and develop logical steps to accomplish each one.

Marketing Strategies

Decide what marketing strategies you will use to promote your company this year. Select the strategies that will work best for you. Here are a few typical strategies you might consider:

- Direct mail campaign
- Customer referral incentive program
- Display ads in trade magazines and/or local publications
- E-commerce
- Radio & television spots
- Personal sales calls to shops

- Billboards & Signage

- Trade show exhibit

- On-site promotional sales event

Of course, you don't have the budget to do everything, but you can do some of these to promote your business.

Once you've chosen your marketing projects for the year, write down the name of each one at the top of its own piece of paper, then develop a logical step by step plan and budget for each. Write down the target date of when you plan to start and complete each project. Have a method in place to keep track of each project's logical steps. For example, use the calendar back-up method; that is where you put the target date on a calendar and then go back on the calendar to add in all the necessary steps to be done on the days they must be done in order to accomplish your project in an organized and timely manner. Once you have thought through the process, put any repeatable plans into a system that can be duplicated in the future. This will save you hours of planning time in the future.

After you have started using a couple of marketing strategies, add more. Keep adding marketing strategies until you've implemented as many of them as you can. The more strategies you use, the better the results.

Finally, make a daily appointment with yourself to do marketing and planning. Schedule this time and make it a solid part

DEVELOP A STEP-BY-STEP PLAN

Once you've chosen your marketing projects for the year, write down the name of each one at the top of its own piece of paper, then develop a logical step-by-step plan and budget for each.

FIND A PRODUCTIVE PLACE TO PLAN

If you can't get the job done at work because of interruptions, find another location for your planning.

of your daily routine. Don't do anything else during this time. Don't answer the phone. Don't receive visitors. Keep this time strictly for marketing and planning. Be consistent and well organized. Pick a time that is the most productive for you. If you can't get the job done at work because of interruptions, find another location for your planning. One client told me the library worked best for him. It was quiet there and he could do research. Whatever works for you, continue to do it consistently to get the results you plan for!

Chapter 7
Develop customer personal relationship systems

I recently called to make an appointment with my physician for a routine checkup required by my insurance. The receptionist asked me when I had last been in and I couldn't remember. "Well," she said, "I can't find you in the system, so it must have been over five years ago so you are no longer one of his patients," she said, "and the doctor is no longer taking any new patients."

My favorite doctor was no longer my doctor! I was sad. I really liked him. This incident reminds me of the reason people usually fall through the cracks. It is through neglect!

It is a well-established fact that you must continually work to stay in contact with your customers to keep their relationship with you strong and healthy and avoid client atrophy. Constant contact does take time and work. The good news is you can dramatically reduce the amount of work you have to do each month by putting your customer contacting efforts into contacting systems. These systems automate your "customer personal relationship programs" (CPR). They keep your customer contacting resuscitated!

DEVELOP RELATIONSHIP SYSTEMS

Dramatically reduce the amount of work you have to do each month by putting your customer contacting efforts into contacting systems.

As you probably know, good systems help you organize any job that needs to be repeated by organizing it into a logical series of repeatable steps. They allow you to put important recurring jobs on automatic pilot. When you think of it, even a cup of coffee can be put into a system. You can make every cup of coffee exactly alike by organizing how you make it, by putting it into a system. You can use the same size cup, the same amount of water, the same type of coffee with the same amount of grounds, and heat it at the same temperature for the same length of time, and this will make every cup of coffee turn out exactly the same.

Most successful companies and all franchises put everything into systems. It is possible for any restaurant, bank, drug store, clothing store, and even used parts business to be put into systems. There is a great book on this subject; it is "The E-Myth", by Michael Gerber. This book can give you some great ideas and tips to help you put your business into productive systems.

Develop customer relationship systems

To develop good CPR systems and make them work, think through the steps of each contacting method you presently use. One CPR method example might be sending thank-you notes to customers who made purchases from you on large ticket items.

Here's how you could put it into a system:

1. Print cards with matching envelopes with your business name and address printed on them. Leave a little space on them to write a short note and add a signature.

2. Have a way to capture the names and addresses of your customers and what they purchased. Also, get the name of the person who sold them the product if you want the note to come from sales staff.

3. At the end of each day, someone at your office writes the name of each customer with their address onto an envelope and adds a first-class stamp.

4. The card is given to the salesman or the owner to sign.

5. The card is sealed and dropped into the mail.

That's it! It's very simple.

A system like this can keep you from losing contact with your customers.

GET THEIR NAMES

Have a way to capture the names and addresses of your customers and what they purchased.

Chapter 8
How to clone your best customers

How to Clone Your Best Customers, double your income, and get a steady stream of new customers buying from you, at little or no cost!

There's a joke about a guy who's out in the middle of a lake in his fishing boat. Suddenly he sees a green snake appear over the edge of his boat with a huge frog in its mouth. The fisherman feels sorry for the frog and whacks the snake on the head with an oar and the snake spits out the frog. The frog swims away happily, but now the fisherman feels sorry for the snake because it didn't get anything to eat. The fisherman doesn't have any food on board, but he does have a flask of whiskey. He gives the snake a drink and it swims away happily. But, a few minutes later the snake returns, but now it has two frogs in its mouth . . .

Okay, okay, I know it is a dumb joke, but it does make a point. The best way to get new customers is for your existing customers to refer someone to you, showing that they appreciate the service you provide.

Here are some rules to get your customers to give you referrals:

Referral Rule #1: *When you recognize and reward certain types of behavior, you get more of the same.* When you get a referred customer, you should make a huge deal out of it. Call and thank the person who sent you the referral. Send them a thank you note and/or a gift. They will refer more and more and more!

Referral Rule #2: *People hang out with their own kind.* The old saying, "birds of a feather flock together" is really true. When one of your *satisfied customers* refers someone to you, the person they referred will probably become another *satisfied customer.* When one of your *best customers* refers someone to you, that referral will become another *best customer.* They will be clones, so to speak, of the ones who referred them to you.

Referral Rule #3: *Referred Customers are Better Customers.* Someone they trust referred them so they come with a certain level of pre-established trust. They are more positive, easier to please and will complain less if something goes wrong.

Referral Rule #4: *Referred customers are less expensive to acquire.* Obviously, it costs less to get a referral than it costs you to advertise. In many cases, it's free.

Referrals are the fastest way to double your business.

Ask your customers to refer new

GET MORE REFERRALS

When you get a referred customer, make a huge deal out of it. Call and thank the person who sent you the referral. They will refer MORE!

ASK FOR REFERRALS

Ask all your best customers to refer one person to you!

customers to you. It's that simple. If you truly have great customer service and you have customers who really love you, they will be glad to send you referrals. Warning; if you're not already getting a few unsolicited referrals from your customers from time to time, it's probably a sign you have some serious problems in your company you need to correct. But don't count on referrals to just happen! It is nice to get the occasional unsolicited referral, but the truth is, you have to work at getting a steady flow of referrals. To do that, you have to put some referral systems in place.

Here is how to put a referral system in place:

1. When a client calls and says you did a great job, thank them and immediately ask for a referral. It's easy and you'll get results. Clients are quick to refer other customers to you when they're happy with you, so don't miss this obvious opportunity.

2. When someone sends a referral, send a thank you note and a gift. Do this even if the referral does not become a customer. The point is, they referred someone to you and you appreciate it. Like the snake with the frog in the example above, this will encourage them to send even more referrals.

3. When a referral actually turns into a buying customer, give the one who referred them something extra in appreciation.

Referral gifts

RECOGNIZE
THOSE
WHO GIVE
REFERRALS

When someone
gives you a
referral, recognize
them publicly!

What do you give as referral gifts? You can give just about anything that people like. It doesn't have to be related to your business but it could be. There are coupons either for your business or another business, dinner at a restaurant, a free lube, movie tickets, etc. Hint: You might be able to work out a deal with a local restaurant, lube shop, or movie theater to get some gifts for free, or at a substantial discount to you for bringing them a new customer. This arrangement could be a win-win situation for both of you. Don't be afraid to be creative.

You could give money as a reward. The size of the reward can be the same for everyone or it can vary depending on the situation. It really depends on what works best for you and what will thrill the customer. I know one business owner who gives $10 for every referral. And he gives the ten dollars in two-dollar bills. Every time the client spends one of the bills, he thinks of him because two-dollar bills are unique. It's a great idea!

Anotherthingyoucangiveisrecognition. When someone refers someone to you, recognize them publicly in your direct mail pieces, in your company newsletter and/or blog. This will encourage others to refer also.

Track Referrals

Always ask new customers how they heard about you. When they say they were referred, write down the name of the person who referred them. Then call or send a note with a gift or, better yet, do both!

Use a Referral Form

- Name _____
  _____

- I was referred by a friend.

- Name of friend: _____
  _____

An excellent book to read on the subject of referrals is ENDLESS REFERRALS by Bob Burg. He describes powerful techniques for setting in motion endless chains of referrals, networking and establishing personal influence.

Chapter 9
How to create sales offers so compelling they can't be refused

A few years ago I decided to sell my house so we could move into a bigger place. We needed more room for our children and I needed room for a new office.

It had been a wonderful house for just a few of us but with four children, the three-bedroom house was bulging at the seams. So I did the typical thing by signing with a real estate broker to sell my house.

Several weeks passed with little results. Even after two open houses, not much happened. Hardly anyone came to look at my house. Here was the problem: There were dozens of other houses also for sale and mine was pretty much lost in the crowd. I was not happy with the slow advertising methods of the traditional real estate people. I decided I could do a lot of advertising for the commission I was paying and I could get better results, too.

I wrote my own ad and placed it in the newspaper. I started it with the headline **"Owner Forced to Leave His Beautiful Dream Home!"** I described the house. I said it had been freshly painted inside and

DESCRIBE EXCITING CUSTOMER BENEFITS

Overcome buyer resistance and procrastination by describing the exciting benefits they'll get in such a ways that they can't help but respond.

out, it looked and smelled new, had new carpet and a new roof. It also had gardens in full bloom with roses, peonies, and other flowers, fruit trees, a greenhouse and a vegetable garden. I said I hated to leave this beautiful home, but I was forced to move because of my job and family situation. I said, "This dream house will be going to a very, very lucky family!!!"

After the ad was placed, my phone rang off the hook! I got over fifty phone calls the day the ad hit, and I sold the house to the first person who called. She begged me to hold it until she could get earnest money down on it. Later, she told me she was sold the moment she read my ad. I had described exactly what *her* dream house looked like. Notice, she had already bought it sight unseen! She was sold by the advertising copy itself that was irresistible. Your ads should do the same thing.

Craft an irresistible offer if you want to make sales

Create a craving. You must overcome buyer resistance and procrastination by describing the exciting benefits they'll get in such a way that they can't help but respond. In other words, describe what they will get as a result of using your products and services. Will their life be better? Will they make more money? Will they be happier?

This is a headline example: *Imagine saving 60% of what you're presently* *paying for new auto parts! The savings on a $100 part puts $60 back into your pocket! Think of what you can do with all the money you will save in a year! Buy a new car! Buy a new boat! Take that dream vacation!*

Solve a pain/worry/problem

Find a problem, agitate it and then solve it. Find out what keeps your customers awake at night. The more in tune with their problems you are, the better you can solve their problems with your products and services.

This is a headline example: *Is your competition about to put you out of business? Are they about to take away the many years of hard work you've invested in your business? DON'T WORRY!!! Our new, 'Pay-You-Back Parts Buying System' will blow your competition out of the water!*

List non-response consequences

Tell them what will happen if they fail to respond to your offer. Some possibilities:

- There is a limited quantity on hand so they must hurry before supplies are gone.

- Prices go up when the coupon expires.

- You can only handle so many calls and some may not get through.

- **Cutoff date**. A legitimate cutoff date will cause prospects to call you now

USE "PROBLEM, AGITATE & SOLVE" FORMULA

Find a problem, (what keeps them awake at night), agitate it, and then solve it with your product or service.

rather than procrastinating. Usually, an odd date will work better because it sounds more legitimate to prospects. Example: *Hurry, coupon expires on Thursday, May 4, at 5:00 pm!*

CONSEQUENCE FOR NOT PLACING AN ORDER

List consequence for not responding to your offer: limited quantity, pricing going up, ending soon.

You know you've created the right kind of offer when your ad causes prospects to drop what they're doing, run to their phone and place an order. In other words, you've created an offer so compelling, it can't be refused.

Chapter 10
Get measureable results by using only direct response advertising methods

"You cannot bore people into buying. The average family is now exposed to more than 1,500 advertisements a day. No wonder they have acquired a talent for skipping the advertisements in newspapers and magazine, and going to the bathroom during television commercials." - David Ogilvy

"The only purpose of advertising is to make sales. It is profitable or unprofitable according to its actual sales." - Claude Hopkins, "Scientific Advertising"

We are bombarded with advertising of all kinds and in many different forms. Billions of dollars are spent each year on advertising. You see advertisements on the sides of buses. They are printed on every kind of consumer product. You hear them on the radio and see them on TV. You see them on billboards, signs, and buildings. They are printed on clothing, shoes, and hats. They come in your mail daily and are in magazines and newspapers. They are all over the Internet.

It can be a puzzle to know what kind of advertising to use! The confusion is easily cleared up when you realize all advertising falls somewhere within two distinct groups: *institutional* advertising and *direct response* advertising. .

Institutional Advertising

Institutional advertising is what you see most of the time. You can easily recognize it because of what it does not have. It does not have an offer, it does not have a call to action, it does not have a cutoff date or deadline, and it doesn't have a way to track its success.

This kind of advertising doesn't try to make an immediate sale but is only about building name recognition. It tries to give you a good feeling or good impression in the hope that you will think of the product or service later when you need or want that kind of product or service. This kind of advertising tries to train you to remember the advertiser sometime in the undetermined future. In other words, it is vague.

Some products that use this kind of *institutional* advertising are soft drinks, beer, automobiles, and clothing. This is a very weak kind of advertising. But big advertising agencies love this kind of advertising and will usually try to get you to

INSTITUTIONAL ADVERTISING METHODS

Institutional advertising does not have an offer, it does not have a call to action, it does not have a cutoff date or deadline and it does not have a way to track its success. **NEVER** use this kind of advertising!

advertise this way. It is expensive and there is no way to accurately track the results. The person selling you this kind of advertising can't be held responsible for zero results. If an ad campaign doesn't increase sales, they blame it on the economy or tell you that you need to run your ads many times for them to work. However, they probably won't work no matter how many times you run them.

Institutional advertising is the most expensive type of advertising. It costs lots of money to sell feelings and name recognition. Name recognition is only possible with a huge advertising budget. Only monster sized companies with bottomless budgets can afford to advertise this way.

Another reason big ad agencies love institutional advertising is because they get to be creative and cutesy to win awards. Madison Avenue type ad agencies live or die by awards which are based on creativity, not results. Many ads have won top awards but did not increase sales. Remember the ad campaign a few years ago for the fast food company that featured the old lady saying, "Where's the Beef?" It won lots of awards, but most people, during the time the campaign ran, couldn't tell you which hamburger chain it was for. Then there was the ad campaign featuring the Chihuahua dog. It also won awards, but sales went down for the company running the ads. During the same time, however, sales for

Chihuahua dogs went up. Institutional advertising proponents don't seem to understand that advertising is meant to get more customers and sell more products instead of simply being an opportunity to be creative.

Direct Response Advertising

DIRECT RESPONSE IS ABOUT RESULTS.

Direct response tells prospects exactly what to do to get a product or service. It gives compelling reasons to respond immediately to an offer. It gets a response! It is also measurable and can be tracked. You can know exactly how much money you make each time you use the direct response method. It's the only type of advertising you should do!

Direct response advertising is different from institutional advertising and you can recognize it because of what it does have. It has features that institutional advertising leaves out. It is all about making sales and getting results. It tells prospects exactly what to do to get a product or service; and it gives compelling reasons to respond immediately to an offer. In other words, it gets a response! It is also measurable and can be tracked. You can know exactly how much money you make each time you use the direct response method.

Direct response advertising is the ONLY method an automotive recycler should use; and any other type of business should too if they want to get immediate, less expensive and trackable results. It will bring the best results for the money you spend. If you want your advertising methods to get measureable results, you must learn how to use direct response marketing. Learn everything you can about it. The more you learn how to use it, the more money you will make from using this method for any advertising you do.

No matter what form of direct response

advertising you use, you will find it far more productive per dollar spent than institutional advertising.

Chapter 11
Why you must guarantee what you sell

It is important for you to have a 100% customer satisfaction guarantee in place, no matter how much it *seems* to cost you.

A while back, a friend of mine told me this story: He decided to call a used parts provider after seeing their advertisement about their good deals and excellent prices. He was very excited after talking on the phone with the helpful and friendly sales person. He was happy that he would save some money and even get the part he wanted delivered to his door. He placed the order for the part and afterward showed the ad to a friend. He bragged to him about the savings and encouraged his friend to take advantage of these same good deals.

Then his part came. He was shocked to discover it was damaged and rusty. He called the company and described the problem. Instead of receiving the positive solution he wanted, he was told they would refund only part of his money. They said it would be too expensive to ship another part to him and explained that they had already spent money shipping the previous part and they would not get back what they had already invested into the part and therefore, could not refund the full amount.

My friend responded by immediately calling the person he had earlier encouraged to buy parts from this company. He warned them not to do business with them. He then stopped by my office and told me about his bad experience and about how sorry he was to have been "ripped off" by "those crooks." He was really unhappy. Who knows how many others he told about his bad experience? Probably lots! Will he ever buy used parts from them again? I think not.

CHEAPER TO KEEP A CUSTOMER

When you factor in all it costs you to get a new customer - the advertising dollars, personal contacting, follow-up hours, telephone calls, and so on - it doesn't take a brain surgeon to know it's much more cost effective to keep a customer than to get a new one.

This is what the parts provider should have done

When my friend called to complain, the parts provider should have immediately worked at his own expense to fix the problem and make the customer 100% happy. Instead of fixing the problem, however, he was only concerned about losing a few dollars and would not replace the defective part. He should look into his parts inspection system to find out how to keep damaged parts from being shipped in the first place.

Lost money

How much money did this parts provider lose by the way he handled this customer? He lost much more than he probably thinks. First, he lost any future sales from this customer over a lifetime. Studies have shown that a delighted customer will buy repeatedly. Secondly, he lost the profit coming from all the people this customer would have referred to him had he been happy. Add up all the potential profits a customer may mean to you, including the initial purchase, future purchases over their lifetime, their referrals, even referral's referrals, and you have a much more serious loss. When you understand how valuable it is to KEEP a customer and how much he is really *worth* to you over a lifetime, you can quickly see how a customer who initially made a one hundred dollar purchase with you can be worth ten, twenty, or thirty thousand dollars in *total customer value*.

When you compare the *expense* of not taking care of a customer, to the *investment* of taking good care of the customer, the answer should be obvious. You should take very good care of every customer! When you factor in all it costs you to get a new customer - the advertising dollars, personal contacting, follow-up hours, telephone calls, and so on - it doesn't take a brain surgeon to know it's much more cost effective to keep a customer than to get a new one.

GO WITH STRONGEST GUARANTEE POSSIBLE

Bend over backwards to produce 100% customer satisfaction. It will pay you back, again and again. Go with the strongest, boldest, best guarantee possible.

Fixing problems is a good investment

Investing a few dollars now in fixing a problem can pay you back many times in the future. However, saving a few dollars now by NOT fixing a problem can cost

*100%
CUSTOMER
SATISFACTION*

Put a 100%
customer
satisfaction
guarantee in place,
no matter how
much it seems to
cost you. If you
cannot provide
a truly great
guarantee for your
products & service,
go find something
else to sell!

you a bundle. Back up your services and products with a well-publicized and clearly posted guarantee. Never let a customer leave dissatisfied. You don't want a single person telling 250 of their friends that you mistreated them in any way. Bend over backwards to produce 100% customer satisfaction. It will pay you back again and again. Go with the strongest, boldest, and best guarantee possible. And, if you cannot provide a truly great guarantee for your parts & service, go find something else to sell!

Chapter 12

Zero-base marketing - it's a way to get free customers

I got a phone call from a client concerned about the response he'd gotten from a mailer we had produced and mailed for him. He had only recently begun to cautiously advertise his company. By cautiously, I mean he was reluctant to spend any money at all on advertising. He had begun his first advertising campaign very modestly. When he first called me, I reassured him it was okay to begin small. In fact, I told him he wouldn't have to spend any money at all on his advertising – if he did his advertising the way I suggested.

So here's what he did

He started with a small, targeted mail list of collision repair shops and general auto repair shops located in his delivery area. He sells both metal (like doors and hoods) and mechanical parts (like engines and transmissions), so this was a logical choice of prospects. We designed a direct mail piece with a good offer and a dollars-off savings coupon attached. We mailed it to the list he chose. Soon his phones started to ring and he was happy with the resulting sales.

But when he looked at his final numbers after the campaign had run its course, he was no longer happy. He figured out how much money he'd spent on his mailing campaign and how much money resulted from the respondents. He was disappointed to discover that he'd only broken even. He had expected much more and called me to complain.

I listened to his concerns and then asked him some questions. I asked him if any new customers called and bought parts as a result of his campaign. He admitted that there had been around thirty or forty first-time customers. But he reminded me that he had still only broken even.

I asked him if he had taken good care of these new customers. Did he make sure they had received a good product and had a pleasant and happy experience with his company? He said he was sure of it.

I then asked him if he thought they might order parts from him again. He thought for a few seconds and said he thought they might.

Let's look at the facts

- 30 or 40 new customers bought a product from him.

- They had a happy buying experience and will probably come back to buy again.

- How much did these new customers

cost him? Nothing! They were free!

- He got 40 new customers and had broken even. The next time these happy new customers buy from him, it is sheer profit!!!

Not bad. Not bad at all!

Smart business owners understand the value of a new customer. They are willing to pay money for new customer acquisition. They are willing to even lose a little money now to gain the lifetime value of a new customer. If a business acquires new customers with their marketing campaign and breaks even, these new customers are absolutely FREE!

After my friend understood the zero-based marketing concept, he decided to look at his marketing campaign as a success rather than a failure. I asked him if he would like to continue to pick up new customers every month without it costing him anything. He said he would! I also asked him how long he thought he could advertise this way? The answer, of course, is FOREVER!

Zero-base marketing is a really great way to grow a company. You do marketing projects, you break even, you pick up new customers each time, you give new customers a happy buying experience with your company; and the next time they order . . . it's PROFIT!

Let's think a little further ahead

Let's see, if we pick up just twenty-

FREE CUSTOMERS

If you break even while utilizing a marketing campaign, and gain some new customers in the process, those new customers were absolutely FREE!

*LIFETIME
CUSTOMER
VALUE*

Profits come from customers who order repeatedly! When you understand this, you know a new customer is a good investment worth paying for in order to receive the lifetime of good business your will receive from them.

five new customers per month for a year, that's three hundred NEW customers. In five years, we've got fifteen hundred NEW customers, and in ten years we've got . . . well, you get the idea!

Of course, it takes a little trial and error to learn how to do zero-base marketing. It's usually best to start out conservatively and expand from there. For you to understand and appreciate the importance of zero-base marketing, you need to understand the lifetime value of a customer. You need to understand your profits come from the customers who order repeatedly! When you understand this, you know a customer is a good investment. You will get a lifetime of good business from him.

When you spend money on advertising and get your money back in sales, - plus, you also get new customers and when the new customers continue to buy, you begin to profit, and if you continue to advertise with this kind of result, you can continue to do this kind of advertising indefinitely.

Chapter 13
Letter writing campaigns

A recycler called me recently and told me about a problem he was trying to recover from in his company. Apparently one of his long time top salesmen got hired away from him by a huge competitor that had recently moved into his area. The really bad part was that the employee did not tell him he was leaving until the day he left. He had accepted the new job several weeks before but had continued to work for him long enough to steal many of his best customers by telling them that he was going to "a better company they should use."

This ploy just about killed this recycler's business! He asked me to tell him what to do. I told him to do two things: First, I told him to write a letter to all his missing customers. Tell them that he sincerely appreciated having their business previously, he missed them, and he very much wanted them back. He should ask them outright what he could do to regain their trust and business. I told him to include a big offer of something free just for them to try him again. Secondly, I told him to follow up the following week with a

WRITE A LETTER TO ALL YOUR MISSING CUSTOMERS

Tell them that you sincerely appreciated having their business previously, that you miss them, and that you very much want them back. Ask them outright what you can do to get them back. Offer them something free just for giving you a second chance. Will this work? You bet!

personal phone call.

Did this work for him? You bet! He had several advantages over the competition. To begin with, he had the "incumbent" advantage of being their first parts provider. This advantage works best if the person has had some kind of personal relationship with the missing customer he can build on. Next, he should work to out-service the competition. The big competitor might claim to give better service, but the truth is they can't. There is no way they can give the personalized kind of service a smaller business or older business can offer. Thirdly, he can develop a Unique Selling Proposition (USP) that the competitor can't match. (See the chapter about developing your USP.) And finally, in time, he can discover and develop smaller niche markets that a large competitor doesn't have time to pay attention to.

Compounding Letter Campaign

A powerful way to make letters work for you is called "compounding" or sending a series of letters to the same prospect. This is the system used very effectively by collection agencies. If the compounding letter method works well for collection agencies helping them to get money from people who don't have any money, think how much more it will work for those who actually do have money!

The first letter is usually a warning and says what will happen if they fail to respond

COMPOUNDING
LETTER
METHOD

A powerful way to make letters work for you is called "compounding" or sending a series of letters to the same prospect. This is the system used very effectively by collection agencies. If the compounding letter method works well for collection agencies, helping them to get money from people who don't have any money, think how much more it will work for those who actually do have money!

by a certain date. The second letter is sent fifteen days later if they don't respond and includes everything the first letter had, but it has a stronger warning. The third letter goes into the mail fifteen days later if they did not respond to the first two and has everything the first two letters had, as well as a more threatening letter. "We have sent you two previous letters and you have still not responded . . ."

Use parts of this idea for your business whenever you are planning a big sale or promotion you want folks to respond by buying, registering, or RSVP-ing to something. You send the first letter that explains the offer and what they get for responding by a certain date. The second letter goes into the mail fifteen days later to those who did not respond to the first. You include everything you had in the first letter but with a different cover letter. You restate your previous offer and give them more reasons to respond by adding some secondary incentives to respond to. Fifteen days later you send the information again with another new cover letter and your "final offer". The new letter says something like this, "Dear so and so, I sent you two previous letters telling you about (yada yada), and frankly I'm puzzled. This is a really great offer and I don't know why you haven't responded." Explain your offer again, with all its benefits and what they will get for responding now. Sweeten the offer by lowering the price slightly, and/or add a promotional item.

You should get a good response from a series of sales letters or a sales letter followed by a personal phone call – whether you have lost a group of customers to a big competitor or not.

Chapter 14
How to write powerful sales letter

If you are like most business owners, you have solid products and services and you have no problem talking about them one-to-one to your customers or prospects. It doesn't matter whether it's on the phone or eyeball to eyeball, you probably know the right words to use and can easily give compelling reasons to buy your products or services. The problem is sometimes people who have absolutely no problem in a personal selling situation suddenly freeze up when they try to write down a sales pitch. They have writer's block and struggle miserably trying to create their sales letter. But there is a way for you to write a powerful sales letter.

I learned this method from a fantastic marketer and communicator, Gary Halbert. He is best known in the marketing world for having written the world's most mailed sales letter. Millions of his letters have been mailed and I'm sure you've probably seen one. . It's the letter that sells directories of family names like "The Jones" or "The Smiths". He has made millions of dollars with that one letter and many other sales letters he has written.

A good sales letter should have the same ingredients as any good advertisement. It must appeal to the interests of the reader, have an irresistible offer, and give compelling reasons for the reader to respond to it immediately.

How to start

To write a great letter, start by forgetting the stuff you learned in school about writing. Begin to record all your sales calls - with the listener's permission, of course. Record your telephone calls, your sales meetings, and your personal one-on-one sales presentations. At first you will be self-conscious whenever you think about the recorder being on. But eventually you will forget about being recorded and that's when the good stuff is recorded and you will begin to persuade the other person to buy what you are selling. That is the dynamic you want to create in your sales letter. Now, go through your recordings and find the ones where you are selling at your wonderful best. Get those recordings transcribed by a typist or use a program like Dragon, which can record and then turn your spoken words directly into text. You can get a free Dragon app for your smartphone and record conversations with your phone in your shirt pocket or with your phone sitting on the counter.

Number & rank paragraphs by value

After your best selling moments have

been converted to text, take a pen and number all the paragraphs. Paragraphs, as you know, are the part of your conversation that contains a single thought or idea. Let's say you have fifty-three paragraphs. Go back and give them another number from one to ten and rank each paragraph in order of its value in influencing the sale of a particular product. Let's say you are selling an extended warranty and mention that it costs very little for the large amount of protection it assures the customer. That paragraph might be assigned an "8". Another paragraph might only get a "2", and so on. When you're done, you will have a sales pitch in print, fifty-three paragraphs long, with each paragraph ranked in order of it's importance on a scale of one to ten.

Organize into three piles

Next, take a pair of scissors and cut all the paragraphs apart and organize them into three piles. The first pile will be the benefits pile with all the paragraphs that describe benefits; The second pile is the fact pile with the paragraphs telling interesting facts about products or services. The third pile is the nothing pile with the paragraphs that don't say anything about products or services and don't advance your sales presentation. Throw out the "nothing pile" and any paragraphs with a rating of five or less. Then rewrite the remaining paragraphs without changing them much. You mainly want to clean them up by taking out the "ums" and "you-knows" and any

FORGET ABOUT BEING CREATIVE AND CLEVER

Don't worry about the approval of some vague other person. Remember, your job is to sell to your customers. Make that your goal.

redundancies. Forget about writing a sales letter. Instead, write a letter as if you're talking to a real person who is interested in what you are selling.

This is an example of a sales letter written with these considerations:

Dear Mark,

I hear you are looking for a Ford 460 big block engine with an extended warranty program. I've got a great engine with all the goodies you asked for, and you won't believe the warranty! It has . . . (Insert highest ranking fact), (then the second highest ranking fact), (third highest ranking fact), (fourth highest ranking fact), etc.

Hey Mark, what about those apples? Maybe now you can see why this particular engine and warranty program is such a fantastic package. There are many benefits you're going to fall in love with! Here are five of them: (Insert paragraph on highest ranked benefit for engine and warranty), (Insert second highest ranked benefit), (Insert third highest ranked benefit), (and fourth and fifth, etc.)

These are just a few of the highlights about how wonderful this engine and warranty are. But actually, Mark, there are many more reasons why it just makes good sense for you to get this engine and warranty and I'd love to explain them to you in person. So here's the deal. I'll give you a chance to think it over for a few days to digest this information. Then I'll give you a call next week and see if you're ready to buy. In the meantime, if you have some questions, or if you are ready to move ahead right now, just give me a call at (000) 000-0000.

Sincerely,

(Your name here).

The best kind of selling communicates facts and benefits in a personal way to the prospect in a way he can receive it, understand it, and respond to it. This goes against the grain of the kind of advertising agency that puts out ads to be clever and to win awards. Forget about being creative and clever.

Remember, your job is to sell to your customers. Make that your goal. You can do it!

COMMUNICATE
FACTS &
BENEFITS

The best kind of selling communicates facts and benefits in a personal way to the prospect in a way he can receive it, understand it, and respond to it.

Chapter 15

Make it easy for customers to quickly place an order with you

Recently, a client called and told me three things. First he wanted 3"x5" post-it notes. Secondly, he wanted his company name and phone number printed at the bottom in blue ink. And thirdly, he gave me his credit card number and said he wanted them ordered TODAY.

I really like it when a client knows what he wants and is ready to buy. So I told him, "No problem" and hung up the phone and prepared his order. It only took a few minutes to produce the artwork he had described. I emailed him a proof, and he immediately replied with an okay to print.

There were several factories that produced these sticky notes so I called the first one on my list. I dialed the phone number. It rang and I got a recorded message. I listened to all the choices, there were several, and I pushed the appropriate button to speak to a sales person. Instead of getting a live person, however, I got another recorded message that said, "I'm sorry, I am presently helping another customer. Please leave a detailed message

EASY ORDERING

There are different kinds of people who have their favorite ways of communicating, so make it easy for them to place their order in every kind of method possible.

at the beep, as well as the time you called, and leave your phone number. We will get back to you as soon as possible."

"BUT, I WANT TO TALK TO SOMEONE NOW!" I said to myself. "I have an order! The art is prepared and I don't want to play phone tag!"

So, I hung up the phone and dialed the same number again. But this time, I pushed the "0" button, hoping to get a live operator who would be able to help me. Someone answered and I told them I was ready to place an order and I wanted a way to do it quickly and simply. I told them I had the artwork, a credit card to pay for it and could get everything to them any number of ways so could we please proceed?

The person on the line said, "I'm sorry, but you will have to talk to a sales person. What State are you calling from?" I told them and they put me on hold to wait.

I waited, and waited, and waited, and every few minutes a recorded message told me my call was very important to them and a salesman would soon be there to help me. Finally, a sales person came onto the line and I quickly told her my story. "I have the artwork approved and can get it to you immediately. I have a credit card to pay, but I NEED to get the order placed, NOW!"

Here's what she said to me. "I'm sorry, but I can't take your order until you fill out a credit application and receive an order number. I will put you through to our

REACH A REAL HUMAN ON THE PHONE

Don't discourage people with "a phone system from hell!" Your customers should be able to place their order by talking to a real human being and simply asking for whatever they need.

96

accounting department so you can get this done."

At this point, I was frustrated and I said to her, "But you don't understand. I want to pay CASH. I don't need any credit, so I don't need to fill out a credit application. I just want to place my order for post-it notes!!"

"I'm sorry," she said, "Our company policy is that we don't take orders without an application and an order number. I will put you through to our credit department so you can take care of that."

I hung up! I called another vendor and a live person immediately answered. They gladly took my credit card number and told me where to email the art. The whole transaction took me less than five minutes to complete! WHAT A DIFFERENCE! WHAT A PLEASURE!

I never, ever called the first company again. I truly wonder how they stay in business!

Here's the rule

Make it as easy as possible for your customers to place an order with you!

- **By Phone**: Your customers should be able to place their parts order by talking to a real human being and simply asking for whatever they need. There are a lot of people who are used to ordering this way and it is their preferred method.. Don't discourage them with a "phone system from hell", if you know what I mean.

- **By Fax**: You can receive orders by fax. Even though just about every business has a fax machine, it is amazing to me how many companies fail to use them to receive orders. Fax machines can take pressure off both your phone system and your counter staff. Consider creating an easy to fill out fax form to give to customers who want to order this way. Have many "check-the-box choices" and a place for customer information, name, phone number, etc., with room for them to describe their parts request. It should have a place for their fax number so you can quickly reply to them, a place for you to put product and shipping prices and a place for their credit card number.

Consider customizing fax forms for your best customers with their personal information printed on them. The easier you make it for your customers to place an order by fax, the more likely they will use it to place their orders. Put somebody in charge of getting those orders priced and placed fast. This will encourage your customers to use this method when they order from you.

- **By Email**: You can take orders this way. Include your counter staff's email addresses on your website, on their business cards, and on your advertising pieces, so people can quickly see how to reach them with parts requests.

- **By Website**: Make sure you have

your website set up so that people can find and order parts from you 24/7 online. More people are ordering just about everything this way. There are lots of companies available now that can help you get your website set up for e-commerce.

Remember, the easier you make it for people to order from you, the more they will do business with you. It's as simple as that!

Chapter 16
Yellow Page advertising

One of the things I like to do as I speak at automotive recycler events across the country is to poll attendees to find out what kind of advertising is being done by those within each group. I consistently find that practically everyone advertises in the Yellow Pages, and many say that Yellow Page advertising is the only advertising they do. Furthermore, most say they believe they pay way too much money for what they get in return. They are usually correct! I intend to help you get more return for your Yellow Page money – in fact, you could save thousands!

I have made it my habit to collect the recycler Yellow Page ads in every city I visit. I now have several folders filled with them. Most of my advice here comes from many years of coast-to-coast research.

Three Things You Automatically Know

When you turn to the Yellow Pages, you automatically know three things about them. First, they are for customers who are ready to buy. Secondly, the customer doesn't know who to buy from, and thirdly the customer can be easily swayed. The

HAVE A BOLD HEADLINE

Most companies make the mistake of using the name of their business as a headline such as "Joe's Used Auto Parts." Use that valuable space for a powerful selling headline such as, "SAVE 40% to 80% off the cost of buying new!"

problem is, most recycler ads are not persuasive! As I look at my collection of recycler ads, most are wimpy – there is nothing about them that sets them apart from each other. Most are like enlarged business cards. This is a problem because consumers want to be swayed to instantly find what they need and get it easily. They need to be persuaded.

The Same Mistake, Repeatedly

Most recycler Yellow Page ads I see are guilty of making the same mistake. First, they use the name of their company as a headline instead of using valuable space to present a huge, attractive customer benefit to catch the eye of the already interested prospect. For instance, each ad has at the top of their display ad something like "Joe's Auto Parts," "Bill's Auto Parts," "Harry's Auto Parts" located above each company's large logo along with their respective phone number and that's pretty much it.

But the thing is, your name and logo have zero pulling power! If there is no offer, there will be no response. If your ad is the same as others, you will be lost in the crowd.

The solution is to use the space to create a direct response selling type of ad. Use strong headlines and subheads that emphasize customer benefits along with a compelling, irresistible offer. Include product photos as well as attractive incentives to drive readers to respond immediately, such as "Mention this ad and receive a free widget or x-amount off your order!"

Have a strong call to action (tell them what to do). Make it easy for them to place an order with you and include as many ways as possible for them to place an order with you by phone, e-mail, website, or fax.

So, where does your logo go? Keep your name and logo small and put them at the bottom of your ad along with your phone number. This allows you to use the valuable space at the top of your ad to promote the biggest customer benefit you company has to offer.

Location, Location, Location!

Make sure your ad is located in the right place in the Yellow Page book. If your ad will be mixed in with others, know that studies have shown people read in a very predictable manner. People read from top left to bottom right, diagonally across the page. Knowing this bit of information will help you understand the importance of ad placement on the page. If your ad is in the top left of the page, it could actually be smaller than the others yet still be the first one seen. Believe it or not, the second best location is at the bottom right of the page. But, don't settle for second best; - you're paying for the ad so get what you want.

Your Rep Won't Like it!

Most Yellow Page sales representative will do everything they can to get you to

HAVE A STRONG CALL TO ACTION (TELL THEM WHAT TO DO)

Make it easy for them to place an order with you. Include as many ways as possible for them to place an order with you by phone, by e-mail, by website, by fax.

USE A SMALLER AD IN A BETTER LOCATION

When you buy a display ad within the Yellow Pages, you also get two free listings from the Yellow Page Company, one in the White Pages and one in the Yellow Pages. Instead of buying a huge display ad, place your smaller display ad into the column under your free listing! Make it the same column width as your free listing. It will be narrow, but you can make it longer.

buy the biggest display ad possible. But size isn't important! It is both the placement of the ad and how the ad is designed that will make the difference to readers.

It is wise to have an outside designer create your ad and not the Yellow Pages sales person. They are designing all your competitor's ads and they don't know anything about selling your kind of products and services. Their goal is to sell you the biggest ad possible and they say the bigger the ad is the more people will see it. They will wrongly tell you you should meet or exceed your competitor's ad size if you want to compete with or beat your competitor.

Know How People Use the Book

First, you need to understand some basics about how people use the Yellow Pages. To begin with, they always look for things alphabetically. If they are looking for auto parts, they first look under the heading of "Auto" and then they look for "Parts." Next, they look at the in-column listings under parts from A to Z.

When you buy a display ad in the Yellow Pages, you also get two free listings from the Yellow Page Company, one in the White Pages and one in the Yellow Pages. Instead of buying a huge display ad, place your smaller display ad into the column under your free listing! Make it the same column width as your free listing. It will be narrow, but you can make it longer. Don't buy a bold headline of your free listing which essentially turns your free listing into a paid listing. Having your display ad located under your free listing will be enough and save you more money.

Also, you don't need to buy the color your Yellow Page sales person wants you to buy. Remember, prospects are already looking in the book from A to Z and they're ready to buy. Having an ad placed in the right location next to your name, plus having it designed as a direct response ad with compelling headlines is enough. If you must have color, use only red because red is the first color people see. Use it sparingly and only on your best offer.

Making Changes

Here are a few suggestions to initiate changes in your current Yellow Page ad. Remember, your sales person wants you to increase your ad size, not go smaller. First, contact your sales person to find out when the closing date is for your Yellow Page ad; but don't tell him you're calling to make your ad smaller. Make an appointment to meet with him ten to fifteen days before that closing date. Have your ad prepared in advance of your meeting with your Yellow Pages representative. When you meet, instruct him or her to write a new contract based upon what you now want. Then have them explain the new contract to you. Make sure both of you understand what headings your ad will go under and that those details are included in the contract. Also, make sure you get your two free listings.

One last important thing, some sales people have gotten so upset when an existing customer decides to go with a much smaller ad because they're losing lots of money that you're now saving!, they may refuse to make the changes saying it's too late. Don't be intimidated. This is why it's important to give yourself plenty of lead-time to deal with this. Be sure to read the small print in your existing contract. Some contracts do state that you must put ad size change requests in writing. If this is the case, I suggest you not only put it in writing, but you also send it to them by certified mail.

Now, just how are you going to spend all the money you're about to save?

Chapter 17
See your customers through their eyes!

There's an old marketing saying, "If you are to sell to John Smith what John Smith buys, you must first see John Smith through John Smith's eyes."

Success in sales is directly related to a salesman's ability to see the customer as they see themselves, and then to serve them accordingly.

HOW CUSTOMERS SEE THEMSELVES

This principle is so powerful yet so simple, many people miss it. People basically focus on themselves - it's an irrefutable fact of human nature. . Babies cry because they want to be changed, fed, cleaned, and cuddled. Watch a bunch of children at a party. Mom comes in with a tray of cookies and says, "Who wants some?" Immediately, the children jump up and down and say, "Me, Me, Me!" They all want to be the first one served. At an adult party, as the host comes in with the tray of food or drink and says, "Who wants some?" Guess what the adults are thinking? Of course, adults don't usually jump up and down and say, "Me, Me", as children do but they do THINK it! They still want to be first

Success in sales is directly related to a salesman's ability to see the customer as they see themselves, and then to serve them accordingly.

one served.

GET TO
KNOW YOUR
CUSTOMERS
AT A
PERSONAL
LEVEL

The better you learn how to serve them, the better you will know how to make sales to them.

ASK THEM

You find out more about your customer by asking them! It's as simple as that!

Use this information to make sales. Get to know your customers on a personal level. The better you learn how to serve them, the better you will know how to make sales. By the way, the first tip I give to someone who tells me they need an immediate spike in sales is to simply phone their customers and speak to them personally. Ask them two questions: "How's your business?" and "Do you need anything?" That powerful tip, which studies have proven to increase sales by 30% or more in a single month, works because it is all about the customer. You are asking how THEIR business is and you are asking if THEY need anything. Your conversation is all about THEM!

You find out more about your customer by asking them! It's as simple as that. At the conclusion of every sale or visit to your business, be sure to ask if they have everything they need. Ask them if there is anything more you can do to improve your service to them. Customer surveys are another great tool. It should ask them about their experience doing business with you and have space for suggestions on how to improve your service.

So, as you begin to see your customers through their eyes, put in your advertising those things that will speak directly to THEIR personal needs. Remember most advertising fails simply because it does not directly and boldly address what the customer wants and needs. The best way to find out what the customer needs is to come right out and ask them.

Chapter 18
Use "human nature" to your advertising advantage

Most automotive recyclers' advertising, and advertising for other types of businesses as well, could be improved greatly if they understood a few basics about human nature. You can make these aspects of human nature work for you when you plan your advertising.

People are self-centered

They care mainly about themselves and what they will get from your company. Unfortunately, most business owners make their ads primarily about themselves. Yes, *they* are self-centered! Instead, you need to answer your customer's biggest question: "What's in it for me?" Focus on how each feature of your advertising actually benefits your customer. For instance, when you feature a new 40,000 square foot warehouse, ask yourself how this benefits your customer. You could say in your ad, "Our new 40,000 square foot warehouse keeps parts in perfect condition for you!" Now, that's a benefit!

People are emotional

PEOPLE ARE SELF-CENTERED

People care mainly about themselves and what they will get from your company.

Their emotions are always present and influence how they respond to advertising. Unfortunately, most automotive recycler ads are emotionally bland. The emotional buying modifiers are curiosity, pride/ego, fear, guilt, greed, imitation, love, rivalry/competition, self-preservation, and variety. When preparing your ad, try to determine what dominant emotional reason will cause your prospect to buy and build your ad around that. Use the other emotional buying motives as secondary reasons to buy. The more emotional reasons to buy you include in your advertising, the better your results will be.

TACTILE PEOPLE

Half of humankind responds best with something in their hands like a flyer, magazine or book (they're tactile) and half of humankind respond best with some electronic form of advertising, such as a smart phone or computer. Use both kinds in order to reach everyone.

Half of humankind is tactile by nature

This means they need something in their hands to touch. They don't respond well to electronic media - even though there are "handheld" versions of them. People read magazines, books, manuals, and other print advertising they can physically hold and respond to. If you have switched away from print advertising totally and opted for electronic forms of marketing, half of your customers or prospects won't receive your communication. You need to do some form of print advertising occasionally to reach the customers or potential customers who aren't reached electronically.

Half of humankind is electronically minded by nature

This means they communicate best through electronic means. They buy online, use social media, and instant messaging. If you are not up-to-speed for this kind of customer or prospect, you are missing half your marketplace..

Half of humankind is analytical by nature

The analytical buyer does not make decisions easily or quickly. They need lots of information before they buy and will read even the tiniest print on your ad. They will go to your website, check references, read every line of your warranty, and talk extensively to your sales person before buying. For this type of person, you must include lots of detail in your advertising.

Half of humankind is impulsive by nature

They are the exact opposite of the analytical person described above. They make decisions quickly and are ready to buy right away. They get bogged down with too much information. They are the ones who respond instantly to all the extra stuff in the checkout lines and respond well to up-sell methods. To reach them, you must tell your entire story quickly and get them to the bottom line fast because they are ready to buy. For this kind of person, the solution is to design your ad with all the small print and details for the analytical person but have well-written headlines and subheads that tell your sales story at a glance. This gets the impulsive buyer to the bottom line quickly so they can make their

ANALYTICAL AND IMPULSIVE

You have to design your advertising to reach both the analytical and impulsive type persons. Include small print and details for the analytical type person but have well-written headlines and subheads that tell your sales story quickly at a glance for the impulsive person.

purchase.

North Americans look at a printed page in a predictable manner

Hidden cameras have tracked eyes scanning a printed page. They have shown most readers start at the top left corner of the page, move down the page moving to the right as they go, and end at the lower right corner of the page. Because of this, they often miss anything printed at top right corner or the lower left corner of the page. If you are placing your yellow page ad on a page with several other advertisers, you want to have your ad placed at either the top left corner or the lower right corner in order to be seen by most readers. You must compensate for those "dead areas" when designing your ads to keep readers from missing important information.

Most of humankind is lazy by nature

You must make your advertising easy to understand and uncomplicated. You must make ordering easy with as few complications as possible. Always overstate the obvious to compensate for lazy minds. Repeat important information a number of ways so they can easily "get it".

So, there you have it! Understand and use the elements of human nature described above to make your advertising projects effective for all types of people.

Chapter 19
Use strategic repetition to maximize advertising impact!

USE REPETITION FOR IMPACT

Ever notice how many times they show the same commercial during a television program? It's often seven or more times. With the high cost of television commercials, you may question the validity of this practice. However, when you grasp what it takes to get people's attention, to break down buyer resistance and to move a customer from inaction to action, you may change your mind. The cold hard truth of the matter is, people have generally grown deaf and blind to TV commercials as well as most other types of advertising. Their eyes may be glued to a TV screen, but there's a good chance their brain is in neutral or thinking about something else, thus, repeated advertising is necessary.

The number of times it takes for an ad to "sink in" is seven to twenty-one times in a condensed period of time. Repetition is required for impact.

Most people are slow to "get it"

Another reason for repetitive advertising is that people retain only about fifteen percent of the information they deliberately concentrate on. This is why advertising people are exposed to, like television commercials and display ads in magazines, can be easily missed.

According to those who understand the psychology of teaching and training, most people only "get it" after they see an ad several times. The number of times it takes for an ad to "sink in" is seven to twenty-one times in a condensed period of time. This is not exactly good news for advertisers on a budget. Obviously, repetition is required for impact.

Not only is repetition important for media like radio and TV, it is also important for print advertising. You may need to place your magazine or newspaper ad in more than one location in the same issue to be most effective. In direct mail, you may need to send the same piece more than once to the same audience for a critical announcements such as telephone number changes, staff changes, or launching new products or services.

Critical information MUST be repeated

You also must repeat important information within every new advertising piece you design. Don't think people will remember what you have said in previous ads. Always repeat what they must know in order to do business with you. Repeat your contact information, staff names & extension numbers. Also, repeat the kinds of products you sell, guarantees, delivery schedules, etc.

Seven times

Repetition is also important within a single ad to help people "see" and re-

REPEAT IN EVERY CAMPAIGN

Repeat important information within every new advertising piece you design. Don't think people will remember what you have said in previous ads.

member important information. When designing a mailer for a direct mail project, for instance, I work to get vital messages in several times. Even though you may think this tactic would be overly obvious to the reader, it's not. Let's say we have a claim like, "Save 40% or more off list." How can I repeat this within the same ad without it looking redundant? Here's how:

1. **Use it in the headline**. This means you use a big headline or bold statement proclaiming it clearly, *"Save 40% or more off List!"* This is where you shout it big and boldly for everyone to see. No problem being obvious about this one.

2. **Incorporate it within your guarantee**. *"Even though you're saving 40% or more off list, our parts are guaranteed with a no-hassle, 110-day replacement warranty!"*

3. **Have it said in a testimonial**. *"I was repairing a rebuilder and bought the replacement parts from Jim's Auto Parts. When I compared the cost, I found that I had saved $997.50. Wow! That's over 40% off list, and extra money in my pocket! - Billy Evans, Evan's Auto Repair Factory, Alton, California."*

4. **Tell a story that demonstrates how easy it is**. *"It's easy to save 40% or more off list. Just pick up the phone and call our toll-free number, it is ..."*

5. **Use it on the "Yes copy" at the top of the order form**. *"Yes, I want to save 40% or more off list. Please enter my*

order for . . ."

6. Use it in your list of bullet points.

- Free Local Delivery
- Nationwide Shipping
- Fast, Friendly Service
- Save 40% or More off List
- Computerized Inventory
- Free Nationwide Parts Locating Service

7. Incorporate it in the P.S. (if it's a letter).
P.S. Don't forget, you will save 40% more off list!

8. Use it on the coupon. *"Save $25 off our already low prices of 40% or more off list, when you buy your next transmission or engine."*

The well-known answer to what makes real estate successful is "location, location, location". In the world of advertising, it's "repeat, repeat, repeat!"

AS MANY TIMES AS POSSIBLE

Repetition is also important within a single ad to help people "see" and remember important information. Work important information in as many places as possible: Headline, guarantee, testimonial, in stories, demonstrations, bullet points, coupons and response devices.

Chapter 20
Since competitors are fishing in your customer pond, you better do something!

Competitors are fishing in your customer pond and using high tech "lures" and delicious "bait," attached to barbed hooks of modern marketing strategies designed to snag your best customers. This is an irrefutable fact in today's world of automotive recycling (and all other types of businesses). Your competitors *are* after your customers! To deny it is crazy and to do nothing about it may be business suicide!

COMPETITORS ARE AFTER YOUR CUSTOMERS!

To deny it is crazy. To do nothing about it may be business suicide. The right kind of customer-friendly advertising will fix the problem!

You can do something about it

The good news is you don't have to stand idly by and let it happen! The right kind of customer-friendly advertising will fix the problem and keep your customers safe from competitor attacks. The key is to do something before it's too late. The problem with most business owners is they procrastinate too long! Don't let this be the case with you!

Truthfully, most tell me they really do *intend* to do "some advertising" for their company but good intentions aren't enough. It reminds me of a story of three frogs sitting on a log. One of the frogs decided to jump. The question is, then, "How many frogs are left on the log?" Although most people answer "two," the correct answer is actually "three!" Just because the frog *decided* to jump off the log doesn't mean it *actually jumped*. In reality, many companies *decide* to put an advertising program into place at the beginning of the year. However, most of them put it off and don't get around to it. They intend to, but it isn't a priority and it gets put off indefinitely. That's why I tell people they must do something. Anything! Anything is better than nothing. But to get results, something has to be physically done.

Customers are sitting ducks

Most recyclers don't do anything to maintain contact with their existing customers other than sending them a statement when something is purchased. Because they don't maintain contact, their customers are easy targets for a competitor who uses any kind of marketing strategy, no matter how lame, to attract them. Studies have shown that for every month your customer fails to hear from you, you lose ten percent of *their* emotional relationship with you! After ten months of not hearing from you, there is no relationship or loyalty left! A competitor fishing in your customer pond can easily snag your customer at this point.

This is dangerous to the success of your business! I warn companies to consistently maintain a good connection and build lasting friendships with their customers or they will surely lose them. At least spend time and money to communicate well with your top customers! Remember the 80/20 rule of business? Eighty percent of a company's business comes from twenty-percent of its customers. Make a list of your "twenty-percenters" and then do special things to show them how much you appreciate them and their business.

REMEMBER THE 80/20 RULE OF BUSINESS?

Eighty percent of a company's business comes from twenty-percent of its customers. Make a list of your "twenty-percenters" and then do special things to show them how much you appreciate them and their business.

Include them in every campaign

Another way to build stronger customer relationships is to include them in every ad campaign you do. Some companies make the mistake of doing advertising projects solely to reach new prospects and leave their regular customers out of the loop. If they do a direct mail campaign, for instance, they are careful to remove all their current customers from the mailing list because they don't want them to take advantage of the money-saving coupons or specials. They are afraid their customers will use coupons intended for reaching new prospects. This is wrong thinking.

Think about it: If you don't reward your customers for doing business with you, they will be more likely to respond to others who do entice them with attractive coupons and offers. I always suggest that existing customers be included in all advertising campaigns aimed at getting new customers in order to maintain, strengthen and keep a good relationship with them.

Your customers are your first responders

Another reason you want to include them in your campaigns is because they already know you and will be the first to pick up the phone when they see your ad. They will help you pay for your campaign. Besides, that little extra you may give to them will pay you back over the long haul in rock solid customer satisfaction, loyalty, and lifetime customer value. Keep in mind you can design your ads to reward both prospects and customers. You can include first-time customer offers as well as deals and coupons for current customers to enjoy.

You MUST do something to get results!

Remember, the very worst thing of all is to simply do nothing to contact your customers in your "pond." Someone said, "If you continue to do what you've always done, you'll continue to have what you've always had;" or, in this case, you may have less and less.

Are you happy with what you have always had? If not, you should use advertising to promote positive change. One of the most logical things to do to keep in touch with customers is to mail them something on a regular basis. If you have a small list, maybe a list of those twenty-percenters, you can probably afford to send

them something with a first class stamp. If you have a larger group to reach, you can mail something at bulk-rate. But again, you need to actually do SOMETHING physically to get any results.

Finally - most companies do very little, if any advertising, so most of the time you are way ahead of most of your competitors if you do ANYTHING. To put it even more plainly, there is one reason and one reason alone that competitors are able to "fish" your customers out of your "customer pond." That reason is inaction on your part. Don't be like the frog still deciding to jump, but he didn't.

Again, DO SOMETHING to let your customers know you are glad to have them.

DO
SOMETHING

Most companies do very little if any advertising, so most of the time you are way ahead of most of your competitors if you do ANYTHING.

Chapter 21
The metamorphosis of a display ad

There are many ways to improve a display ad. Many ads I see really DO need improvements! The following steps are the usual ones I go through to improve a typical display advertisement. In fact, using any of these steps will likely give you the "edge" over most of the ads you see today. Too many ads miss important selling essentials.

Original

A to Z Used Auto Parts

A-Z

555 Pine, Belmond, WA 09080

Phone: 555-0000

(#1) The **original**. What you typically see in the "Used Auto Parts" section of the yellow pages or on the pages of most recycler periodicals is an ad that is basically nothing more than an enlarged business card with the company name, logo, address, and phone number. That's it! It's dull and boring. There's nothing there to make a sale! It's what we call in the advertising business, "me too" advertising.

Headline Is Added

2

You Will Save 40% To 80% Off OEM Parts

A to Z Used Auto Parts

555 Pine, Belmond, WA 09080

Phone: 555-0000

(#2) Add a **headline**. A headline is usually the most important improvement you can make to an ad. A headline that says, "You Will Save 40% to 80% Off OEM Parts", offers a huge customer benefit and corrects the biggest mistake made by most recyclers, which is to use the name of their company as a headline. Unless your name is something descriptive like, "Cheap Dependable Parts-R-US," or you are a major company giant who has previously spent gazillions of advertising bucks on name recognition, there is no selling value to your name.

Free Delivery Added

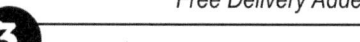

You Will Save 40% To 80% Off OEM Parts

A to Z Used Auto Parts

555 Pine, Belmond, WA 09080

Phone: 555-0000

(#3) Add the words, "**Free Delivery**". That's another big improvement that can be made to most ads. Give something away by using the word, "free". The word "FREE" is the most powerful selling word in existence and should be used as much as possible to improve the pulling power of any ad. Don't make the mistake of assuming that everyone knows what you offer for free. One company owner realized that his sales staff usually gave out a lot of technical information while speaking to customers on the phone. Customers expressed their appreciation for this help, so he capitalized on this by referring to his counter staff as "Parts Experts". Then he added this free customer benefit to his advertising by saying "Free Technical Support! Our Parts Experts Are Here To Help You!"

(#4) Add a **coupon**. Adding a coupon is another way to give something away free as well as a way to make your ad a keeper. It's my personal opinion you should use coupons as much as possible. Most customers forget to use them at the point of purchase; only about 3 percent remember to use them, but coupons dramatically improve the response rate because people keep the ad because of the coupons.

Call To Action Added

(#5) Add a "**call to action**" statement. Most ads fail to tell readers what to do. Don't assume people know what you want them to do. If you want them to call, say so. If you want them to stop by your business, say so. If you want them to write a check, say so. If you want them to fill out a form and mail it, say so. If you want them to ask about your extended warranty program, say so. People need to be prompted into action.

Toll Free Number Added

You Will Save 40% To 80% Off OEM Parts

A to Z ◀A▶Z *Free Delivery!*
Used Auto Parts

555 Pine, Belmond, WA 09080

Call Us Today!

Local: 555-0000

Toll Free: 800-555-0000

C O U P O N

$25 Off
Your First Order

(#6) Add a **toll-free phone number**. This change will make a big difference to customers who don't want to pay for a long distance phone call. In fact, if your ad appears in the same place as your competitor's ad, such as in the Yellow Pages, your ad is competing with theirs. Many readers will instantly scour all the ads looking for companies with toll-free telephone numbers and will ONLY call them. . A few extra cents for the call is worth it.

(#7) Add a **guarantee**. This helps eliminate buyer fears and buyer resistance. You should use strong guarantees as much as possible. This is not only a good business practice, but it goes a long way to combat used part buyer resistance.

(#8) Add a **testimonial**. This is a very

powerful addition. A testimonial adds proof to back up seller claims and adds credibility. I frequently add a picture with the person's name and the name of his company to reinforce the credibility of the testimonial.

(9) Add a second color. Red, is the best color because it is the color of blood and get's attention first. Use it to highlight important things you want buyers to notice within your ad. In our example ad you could use red for the headline, "You Will Save 40% To 80% Off OEM Parts", red for "Free Delivery" and coupon offer money amount, "$25" draw the eyes to those areas.

(10) Add full color. Use colorful backgrounds, photos and illustrations to make your ad pop.

Chapter 22
Coupons really do make a difference in sales!

Use as many of them as you can!

You see coupons everywhere these days for just about every type of business. Just when I think I've seen everything, I spot yet another type of business using coupons to sell its products and services – even a local funeral home. Who would have ever thought?

Coupons are actually good for any type of business when used correctly. Coupons can instantly draw a prospect's attention to an otherwise boring advertisement and make it stand out in the crowd. In the case of direct mail, a great value added coupon can keep the advertiser's investment from being quickly tossed as their prospect sorts his mail over the trash.

Coupon fear

I've found, however, a few recyclers are simply afraid to use coupons because they are afraid of giving something away. They're concerned they might get a landslide response and then be forced to give away a ton of their hard-earned money. But let's be serious, it actually would be GREAT to

ATTENTION
GETTING
COUPONS

Coupons can instantly draw a prospect's attention to an otherwise boring advertisement and make it stand out in the crowd.

get a landslide response and be forced to give away a ton of coupon money because it would represent a lot of sales!

People intend to use them, but forget

Studies show that only three percent of those who clip coupons and intend to use them actually remember to redeem them at the point of purchase. This is because people get distracted with the other details of their purchase, and simply don't remember to use them. Here's my experience: A while back, I received a coupon in the mail offering $10 off my next lumber purchase at a home supply store located several miles beyond my favorite store. I didn't want to miss the ten dollar savings so I drove the extra miles to get some lumber for a project I was working on. I wandered around the store finding what I needed and even helped the person at the checkout counter find all the little bar codes affixed to the lumber. I paid with a check, loaded the lumber onto my truck, and was halfway home before I remembered the savings coupon still in my shirt pocket!!! It was too much trouble for me to turn around and go back. I felt stupid for forgetting, but realized firsthand why most people do forget to use coupons even though they plan to.

For this reason, some business owners actually count on their coupons not being used and include them in their advertising only for the purpose of turning their ads into "keepers." But this is not right thinking because coupon usage makes happy customers and each redeemed coupon represents an actual sale. Smart business owners see the big picture of coupons being part of their customer acquisition and retention program. It's part of growing a healthy business. They design them to "buy" new customers, make them happy, give them a pleasant buying experience, and then entice, in fact reward, them to come back and buy repeatedly.

Encourages customer loyalty

I encourage every business to use lots of coupons in every advertising project. But, I find lots of resistance. If I do manage to talk them into using coupons, they want to put lots of fine print such as "for new customers only" or they want to remove their current customers from the mailing list so only their prospects will see the coupons. But this is wrong thinking! They should always include their customers on the list and reward them for their faithfulness. Also, competitors are constantly putting coupon offers in front of their customers and if they don't allow their current customers to use their coupons, they may lose them to competitors.

Do you know the lifetime value of your customers?

Most businesses are busy trying to get NEW customers without understanding that it is less expensive and more rewarding to keep their present customers than

COUPONS MAKE SALES AND ENCOURAGE LOYALTY

Coupon usage makes happy and loyal customers and each redeemed coupon represents an actual sale.

to get new ones. To understand this, you will need to know the average sale per customer, the average number of times per year they purchase, and how many years an average relationship lasts. You may not know the exact amount of acquisition and maintenance costs, but I recommend estimating on the high side. The number of referrals will vary over the life of a customer based on the industry.

Example:

- Average Sale: $100

- One sale per month for a year: $1,200.00

- 10 years average relationship: $12,000.00

- Acquisition cost: less $100 = $11,900.00 remaining

- Maintenance cost: less $100 = $11,800.00 remaining

- 5 referrals and their value - $59,000.00

Those who really understand the Lifetime Value of their existing customers will work their hardest on customer retention and customer service programs. They will make an effort to stay in touch with them, rewarding them with coupons!

Different coupon offers

There are lots of different ways to design coupon offers. You can offer money off such as, "$25 off any transmission."

Or you can offer a percentage off such as, "10% off any engine."

You can offer something for free with a purchase, such as, "Get a FREE tee-shirt with any purchase," or "Get a FREE dinner & movie with the purchase of any front clip".

Then there are many combinations like: "Buy one and get one free" or "Get two for the price of one." Or, "Buy two and get one free," or even "Buy three and get the fourth one free."

Then there are "apples/oranges" combinations, which means if they buy one thing they get a different item at a discount, such as "Buy any front clip and receive 50% off any pair of doors".

Coupons really do make a difference in sales. Consumers clip them, save them and use them. Coupon usage in America is huge. Consumers have come to expect them and look for them so don't forget to include coupons in your next advertising project.

Discount coupons can dramatically improve your advertising response rate if they are designed correctly. Here are some tips on how to make them work for you:

1. Make coupons look like coupons. Put a thick dashed line around them, or around the entire ad, so there is no confusion. Avoid fancy borders and certificate type borders. The dashed line invites the customer to cut it out.

COUPONS ARE EXPECTED

Coupons usage is huge in America! Consumers have come to expect them and look for them, so don't forget to include coupons in your next advertising project.

2. Make the offer the main focus. If the offer is "$25 off" make sure the "$25 off" is the biggest thing they see. Don't make it hard to see the good deal by making your offer obscure.

3. Make it obvious the coupon should be clipped. Place the icon of scissors near the top left-hand corner of the border.

4. Include a picture of the item being offered.

5. Include an expiration date and any rules or exceptions at the bottom such as, "In stock orders only - one coupon per order."

6. Include your company name, location and phone number on the coupon because clipped coupons often get separated from the rest of the ad and consumers forget what store they are from.

7. Place coupons on the outside edge of the page for easy removal.

8. Place the coupon so it is on the on the back of the mailing label. If you do this, every coupon returned will have the name and address of those who turned them in. This works well for postcard type mailers but is not always best for multi-page mailers where the coupon would end up inside the publication and out of sight to the receiver. If you must locate your coupon inside, then announce it on the outside. Use teaser copy or a "flash" on the outside that says something like, "See Money Saving Coupon Inside!"

Chapter 23
How to get lost customers back

"Most companies today don't know how many customers they've lost, much less attempt to bring them back. The average company loses 20 to 40 percent of its customers each year. Nearly half of them don't even know why the customers left or attempt to do anything about it."

Austin Business Journal

A well-known survey demonstrates why businesses lose customers: 1% die, 3% move away, 5% switch because a friend or relative introduces them to their preferred merchant, 9% switch because they believe they've found a better product or service, 14% leave because of product or service dissatisfaction, and the most, a whopping 68%, leave because of neglect!

Some of the things on the above list you obviously can't do anything about. For instance, you have no control over customers who die or move away. But, on the other hand, you most certainly *can* do something about the 14% who have stopped using you because of some problem they had with your products or services. The answer is so simple it's almost ridiculous.

Contact them! That's it! Call them, go to their place of business and visit with them face to face or write them a personal letter, - but don't use a form letter!

And what are your chances of success when you use this approach? According to research from Marketing Metrics, a Paramus, N.J., based consulting firm, they say: "Your chances of successfully selling to a former customer is 20 to 40 percent. That's significantly higher than the 5 to 20 percent chance you have of selling to a new prospect. Your chances are better, because former customers already know you and what your products or services can do. Plus, you know them. You know their past buying behavior, so you have a significant advantage over competitors who don't have this information."

So, when you contact your prodigal customer, here's what to say to them: *Is there anything wrong? I want to know.*

And, of course, you really *do* want to know the answer to this very important question. Then you can be aware of problems and fix them.

Why does this contacting method work? Think about it for a moment and ask yourself these two questions: first, did you ever stop using someone's products or services yourself because you had a negative buying experience with them? And secondly, did they ever call you and ask why you had stopped ordering from them? If you are like most company owners, the

CONTACT LOST CUSTOMERS!

The average company loses 20 to 40 percent of its customers each year. Nearly half of them don't even know why the customers left or attempt to do anything about it. The answer is ridiculously simple, just contact them! By personally contacting every inactive customer or prospect you have, a wonderful thing will occur; you will get most of them back!

answer to the first question is *yes* and the answer to the second question is *no*.

Regarding the second question - let's say they did notice you'd stopped using them and they did call and ask you what the problem was. They were very humble and very sorry about the problem you had with them. Let's say they asked you very earnestly and very sincerely what they could do to fix the problem and asked for your business back. Would you give their company another shot? If you are like most people, you probably would! Quite frankly, after their call, you'd undoubtedly have a deeper level of buying relationship with them than you had previously.

Here's what you can do to get back the 68% who have left because of neglect. To begin with, let's consider the very real possibility many of them didn't leave intentionally. Some kind of personal event in their life or business occurred to distract them from buying from you for a while. They may have even lost your address or phone number, but the results were the same, they didn't call to place an order from you.

So, here's what you do. Use the exact same approach as described earlier. Call them up and say: *Is there anything wrong? I want to know.*

Guess what usually happens next? They are sorry they've completely forgotten about you for so long, especially since you're so concerned about them.

Then something amazing happens next. The law of reciprocity intercedes and they become even more eager than you to begin doing business with you again. But now it's at a deeper level than before. You've just cemented your relationship with them.

So, just by personally contacting every inactive customer or prospect you have, a wonderful thing will occur; you will get most of them back! Once they start purchasing from you again, there is a high probability they will actually become the most loyal and profitable customers or clients you will ever have!

So, what are you waiting for? Go get those lost customers back!

Chapter 24
How to get and use powerful testimonials

Testimonials are very important for promoting your business and selling your products and services. What others say about you has a greater impact than what you say about yourself. Testimonials are the most powerful way to sell. You can increase the response to your advertising dramatically by adding testimonials. If you want to get and keep the marketing edge, use testimonials!

TESTIMONIAL POWER

What others say about you has a greater impact than what you say about yourself. Testimonials are the most powerful way to sell.

Proof of credibility

One good reason to use testimonials is they are proof of credibility. What you say about your business, products and services means far less to consumers than what another consumer says. Testimonials prove in a way that you can't, that your claims about your business have credibility.

Buyer fears

Testimonials reduce or alleviate a buyer's fears. Let's face it, there are people who are afraid to buy and use recycled parts. They are afraid the parts will fail and they'll be stuck. They're afraid about the quality of the parts, or they are afraid you won't deliver on time. There are other things they're afraid of that stop them from buying, too. You can assure customers but your words don't have the same impact as the words of a satisfied customer. Let's take the first fear – that the parts will fail and they'll be stuck. To address that fear, you can print a customer testimonial that says, "Hi, I'm Troy Ferguson of Troy's Auto Body & Repair. I have bought used recycled parts from Harry's Auto Parts for seven years. The parts arrive on time, in good condition, they fit, and they're guaranteed! I like using Harry's Parts because they're OEM parts that have been carefully removed from late model salvage. They're parts I can trust. Harry's has saved me thousands of dollars. They have always helped me get what I need." You could say these things about your company yourself, but they would never have the powerful impact of a direct quote from a satisfied customer.

Gather customer testimonials for all aspects of your business. For delivery: "Harry always delivers to me fast." For customer service: "Harry is there for me in my hour of need. It was 4:45pm and I had a job to get out when I called Harry's. They were about to close, but they stayed late and got me the part I needed. They saved my day!" For price: "I saved $230 on the engine I needed when I got it from Harry's. I added up the savings over the last six months and found that I'd actually saved a whopping $16,230 dollars on parts! Not

GET LOTS
OF THEM

Gather customer testimonials for all aspects of your business.

only are we going to Disneyland, but we're paying off two credit cards - thanks to Harry's!"

Be specific

To get maximum impact from Testimonials make them specific: "I saved $497.50." Avoid using words like "great" or "quality" or other non-specific phrases like, "They really care." These words are non-specific and almost worthless. Always include details because details give credibility. "I saved $497.50" is better than "I saved money" or "I saved about $500.00" – which is only slightly better.

Answer an objection

Answer an objection by including a testimonial like: "When I thought about using recycled parts I was really nervous. I was afraid I would be shipped junk and would be stuck with it. But I have learned first-hand that Harry's Recycled Parts ships nothing but the finest OEM parts. Before I bought, I personally toured Harry's and saw how each part was professionally removed from late model vehicles using state-of-the-art equipment and technology. I saw how each part was cleaned, tested and inspected before it was shipped. I found I don't have to worry about being stuck. Harry's puts an inspection sticker on every part with the name and phone number of the inspector so I can call if there is a problem. I love the 100%, no-hassle, money-back guarantee with a 101-day-warranty on every part." -

Greg Gimble of Gimble's Auto Repair

Prove what you claim

Prove a Claim: "On Saturday afternoon at two minutes to five, I had a problem installing a part. I called Harry's and explained my problem. I knew they were probably closing and would tell me to call back on Monday. But they didn't! The guy stayed on the phone for thirty-five minutes and helped me figure it out. He even gave me his home phone number in case I ran into more trouble. I still can't believe how helpful and patient he was!" - Tim Evans, Evan's Auto Body Shop.

Keep it real

When you use testimonials - NEVER make up testimonials!! You could get in deep water legally if you do. The truth is, you better be getting some wonderful testimonials unsolicited or it's a sign you have customer relationship/sales problems you need to fix immediately.

Ask for them!

Ask your customers for testimonials. When someone tells you they liked your service or appreciated doing business with you, ask them if they mind putting it in writing for you. Most customers are very happy and willing to do this. But, amazingly, many businesses never think to ask for testimonials.

When customers see you use testimonials in your advertising, they will be

ASK FOR CUSTOMER TESTIMONIALS

When someone tells you they liked your service or appreciated doing business with you, ask them if they mind putting it in writing for you.

inspired to send you one, too. The more you use testimonials, the more you get.

Develop and use a testimonial questionnaire

Never leave testimonial writing totally to the customer because most won't know how to write one and it will keep you from getting something useless. When someone offers to give you a testimonial, use a questionnaire to collect the information needed. Draft their testimonial from the information they supplied, then send the final draft to them for their approval and signature, so you can use it as is. Once they approve of what you write, their testimony is genuine and still theirs. Because of this, you will have a valuable, powerful tool to use in your advertising.

Sample Testimonial Questionnaire

My name is _____

My street address is _____

I live in the town of _____

I own my own business _____

My age is: _____ 18-30 _____31-40 _____41-55 _____56-up

My experience with the staff of (name of your company) during the entire process of buying parts was: (please be specific) ___

_____

_____

_____

_____

_____

WRITE TESTIMONIALS FOR THEM

Never leave testimonial writing totally to the customer because most won't know how to write one and it will keep you from getting something useless. When someone offers to give you a testimonial, use a questionnaire to collect the information needed to create the testimonial for them.

_____

_____

The thing I like best about (name of company) is: _____

_____

The biggest reason I chose (name of company) _____

_____

Other comments: _____

_____

_____

Chapter 25
How to get published in the newspaper

This is how you can get thousands of dollar's-worth of FREE advertising! There are sections of the newspaper reserved only for news features. You can't buy advertising space there for any price. But you *can* get your story featured there for free!

Paul Hartunian is an absolute master at getting free advertising. Articles about him and his products have been featured in top publications across the country. He puts out news releases so exciting that reporters flock to his door. His news releases are usually submitted to small papers hungry for public interest news stories. Then these stories are picked up and published by bigger papers and national publications. As a result, he's been featured as a guest on **Oprah** and The **Tonight Show**. These stories have translated into incredible free exposure and tremendous product sales for him.

He bought the Brooklyn Bridge!

Here is just one example of how Paul Hartunian has gotten free news coverage.

One day he was driving home from

GET FREE ADVERTISING WITH NEWSPAPER ARTICLES

There are sections of the newspaper reserved only for news features. You can't buy advertising space there for any price. But you can get your story featured there for free! Write and use exciting news releases about your business!

work and noticed repairs being done to the Brooklyn Bridge. Workers were tearing up the old planking and replacing it with new planking. He called the person in charge and asked what they were planning to do with the old planking. He was told they were planning to take it to the dump. He asked them if he could get rid of it for them. Not only did they agree to give it to him, but they actually delivered it to his door!

The next thing he did was arrange to have the planks cut up into small pieces. He also asked a printer to print a card with the following line, "**A piece of the Real Brooklyn Bridge!**" Then he glued a small piece of the Brooklyn Bridge planking to the front of each card. Next, he wrote a news release with a headline at the top that said, "Man discovers a way to legally sell you the Brooklyn Bridge!" Then he told the story on the rest of the card.

His news release was not only in papers from coast to coast, but he was overwhelmed with requests for interviews. Needless to say, he sold zillions of dollars-worth of the Brooklyn Bridge!

Get published

Maybe you're not trying to get something sensational printed, but you can still get copy published in the paper. It's very easy to do and there are a number of good reasons to do this. First, an article in the newspaper about your company builds credibility and exposure for you and helps diminish buyer resistance to your products and services. You can also use the printed articles to promote your business by including reprints along with other things you send to your prospects. When they see positive articles written about you and your company in the newspaper, it translates into sales.

Write a news/press release

Because newspapers get many news releases, it's good to know how to write one that will get published. If you want something in the newspaper, you need to do more than just send a news release to them, you must to do some preliminary work. Begin by calling the newspaper to find out who's in charge of press releases. This will allow you to send your press release directly to the right person and bypass the gatekeeper. The gatekeeper is the person at the newspaper who screens the mail. You don't want your news release to get stopped at the door. Call back and ask to speak directly to the right person. Tell them about your project and that you are sending a press release. When you send your release, write on the front of the envelope, "To the attention of" and write the name of the contact person. It will go directly to them and not get held up in the normal screening process.

Use the standard format

Most newspaper publishers want news releases to be written in a standard format

NEWSPAPER ARTICLES GOOD FOR BUSINESS

A well written newspaper article about your company builds credibility and exposure for you and helps diminish buyer resistance to your products and services.

as described below.

1. Use letter-sized white paper and a standard 12 point font such as Times Roman or Helvetica. Don't write your news release on your letterhead or on fancy paper. Make it very plain and use only black ink.

2. Put contact information at the top of the left side of the page. Type your name, phone number, and address there. They want it at the top so they can easily find the information and know who to contact for confirmation and/or to receive additional information.

3. At the top center of the page write the words, "For Immediate Release."

4. Above the first paragraph of your article put a *news* headline, not a *sales* headline. This is a news announcement and not a sales letter. You have to tell absolute facts to the newspaper. They are looking for interesting *news* stories. They don't want to be conned into printing a sales promotion for your company. Use something simple and factual such as, "New Approach to Auto Parts."

5. Type it double-spaced. Newspaper publishers want it this way to make any editing easier for them.

6. Start with your most important information; telling the main thing about your product, project, new employee, event, or whatever it is you are announcing. Use the

inverted pyramid style of writing which is to write the article so that the most important information is first and the least important information is last, then the editor can chop from the bottom if he needs to shorten it.

7. Insert photographs or disk into the envelope with the press release. If there is a photo to go along with your article, don't staple it or otherwise attach it to the letter. Be sure to label photos and disks with your name and address in case you want them returned or in case they get separated from the letter. If you want materials returned include a stamped self-addressed envelope for the convenience of your news contact.

8. Mail your press release materials to the attention of the person you spoke to on the phone. This will get your piece directly into the hands of the right person where it is most likely to get used.

9. Write a thank you note when your article appears. Remember, you really do appreciate their use of your article. You want to build a good personal relationship with them for the future.

USE REPRINTS TO PROMOTE YOUR BUSINESS

You can also use the printed articles to promote your business by including reprints along with other things you send to your prospects. When they see positive articles written about you and your company in the newspaper it translates into sales.

Chapter 26
Ethics will make or break you

Bad ethics can totally undermine an advertising campaign. The following story will illustrate how ethics can make or break your advertising campaign.

The case of the failed mailer and the riled recycler

"Harry the Recycler" decided to do a direct mail campaign because his business was slow and he wanted to get his phone ringing. I helped him develop a direct mail piece for his company that had all the right selling ingredients in it. It was powerful and eye-catching. I mailed it to a great list of prospects in his area.

He got a disappointing response when no one called. He was mad! He called me and complained. I told him I would look into it and see if I could figure out why his mailing campaign didn't work well for him.

By the way, here are a few reasons a direct mail campaign could fail:

1. The direct mail piece is boring

2. It's "me-to" advertising with no Unique Selling Proposition (USP)

3. It doesn't feature benefits attractive to the receiver.

4. It has no offer to respond to

5. It has no guarantees to counteract buyer resistance

6. It has no coupons to reward buying

7. It has no deadlines as a reason to act now

8. It's claims are not backed up with proof so there's a credibility problem

9. It has no call to action. (It asks nothing, so gets nothing.)

10. It hits at a bad time, such as during a storm or on a weekend.

11. It's sent to a bad mailing list with the wrong prospects

12. It gets lost by the Post Office; - this is rare but does happen

13. It hits the same time as a competitor's mailer and the competitor has a better offer or coupon

14. A bad reputation precedes it

So I checked out every possibility. I knew the mailer was put together correctly with all the right selling ingredients. It was not a boring piece. It had a great offer along with coupons and a strong call to action. I knew the mailing list was right. I knew it had actually gone into the mail system and was delivered. There was no storm to interfere with the response. So the problem had to be somewhere else. Finally, I got on the phone and called a few of the business owners that the piece was mailed to. Bingo! I quickly discovered the problem. A bad reputation had preceded it! The problem wasn't the mailer, it was the sender!

Unethical, to say the least!

Everyone I called told me the same thing. This person was highly unethical in his business practices. People told me over the phone that they would never do business with this person again because, "He's a crook!" A few people got mad at me the instant they heard this person's name. I heard story after negative story. It was exhausting to listen to!

After getting off the phone, I knew only one mailing campaign would work for this company: a mailer with a huge headline at the top that said . . . UNDER NEW OWNERSHIP!

Negative consequences

Here's the point you must learn from this: in order to build a strong company that will last for years, you MUST be 100% ethical! No exceptions! Unethical people may be successful for a while, but the problems they make will eventually catch up with them. What they did in their past will finally produce the negative consequences that follow such practices and their business will not survive.

Why are some businesses owners unethical? Because they think it saves them

AVOID NEGATIVE CONSEQUENCES

In order to build a strong company that's going to last for years, you MUST be 100% ethical! No exceptions!

money! They are dead wrong. It is absolute suicide to be unethical. The truth of the matter is unhappy customers will shout to the world that you are unfair and unethical. They will complain to everyone they know about it. They will even tell people they don't know! Every time your name is mentioned, they will react negatively and probably publicly. It doesn't take many unhappy customers to literally destroy a business.

Keep customers happy!

Do everything you can to keep your customers happy. If you get a really bad apple, give them their money back anyway. Ask them if you can do anything else to make them happy. Then resolve privately to fire them as a customer. You don't have to do any future business with them but you don't want them to leave unhappy and be spreading a bunch of garbage about you.

Be a promise keeper!

So many businesses don't live up to their promises. You must live up to all your promises! Here's the secret to keeping promises. Only make promises you *CAN* keep and don't make promises you *CAN'T* keep. This is a simple and easy to understand business principle. For example, if you describe the condition of a used part to a customer and it arrives differently than what you said, your customer will be mad. If you say a part will ship to him today, and you don't ship it until tomorrow, he'll be mad. On the other hand, if you describe the part accurately, describing any damage, there won't be a problem. He'll be expecting what he gets. If you tell him you can't ship it until tomorrow, he won't be angry with you. Always explain why you can't do something!

Only positive surprises, please!

No one likes negative surprises. If you are going to surprise someone, make it a happy surprise. If you tell your customer you don't think you can ship his part today, but then discover you actually can, you will be a hero.

Being ethical is not only good business; it will bring you lots of referrals and even help you sleep at night!

ONLY MAKE PROMISES YOU CAN KEEP!

And never make promises you can't keep. This is a simple and easy to understand business principle.

NO ONE LIKES NEGATIVE SURPRISES

If you are going to surprise someone, make it a happy surprise. If you tell your customer that you don't think you can ship his order today, but then discover that you actually can after all, you will be a hero.

Chapter 27
Developing a borrow file for fresh ideas

In advertising, you do NOT need to be original! You can let others create for you!

Companies pay lots of money for original ideas but you don't need to pay for ideas and you don't need your ideas to be original! There are already great ideas all around you can legally borrow from.

When you find something interesting, put it in a file that you can draw ideas from later. Use this file to create your own advertising. You need to understand your borrow file is for ideas only!

You cannot steal or plagiarize copyrighted material from someone else's advertising but when you get dry on ideas, you can go to your borrow file to get your creative juices flowing by looking at what others have done.

Then you can custom tailor it to your own specific needs. That is perfectly legal. Idea borrowing is done all the time and it's not morally or ethically wrong. No one can copyright ideas or formats. This is why you see so much imitation in music, fashion, TV

YOU DON'T NEED TO BE ORIGINAL!

Companies pay lots of money for original ideas but you don't need to pay for ideas. And you don't need your ideas to be original; there are already great ideas all around you that you can legally borrow from.

shows, diets, movies, computer technology, consumer products and many other things.

These are a few places to look for the materials for your idea file:

Junk Mail

That's right. The first place to look for ideas is in your own mailbox! The US Mail is a gold mine of free ideas you can capitalize on! Begin by thinking differently about junk mail. It is a great resource for free ideas if you know how to glean from them! Big agencies pay millions of dollars each year to top writers and graphic designers who produce that mountain of junk mail flooding your mail box. Even though most of it is fluff and deserves to go into the trash, you will find an occasional nugget you can use. Keep examples of the ones that grab your attention and make you want to buy. Borrow those ideas to produce your own ads.

Use your own headlines and your own photos to make a new piece that is totally yours. After you've done this for a while, you'll develop an eye for what's good, what's bad and what you can use. Remember, the best stuff grabs the reader's attention and answers his biggest self-interested question of "what's in it for me?" It also compels him to act. Keep in mind that there is value in bad stuff, too. Figure out why the bad ones didn't get your attention and begged to be trashed. As a helpful exercise, rewrite and redesign the bad advertisements.

MANY SOURCES ALL AROUND YOU FOR IDEAS

Always keep your eyes peeled for ideas from anywhere you happen to be for your borrow file. You'll find them all around you. Look at ads in your social media postings, local penny shopper, on billboards, on restaurant tables and even in hotels.

Magazines

There is a multitude of great ad ideas to be gleaned from magazines of all kinds. Whenever I go to the grocery store or bookstore or I'm at the airport, I look at magazine racks to see what's new and different. If you do this, don't just stick with the magazines you like, but check out others, too. Find ideas in one industry that you can use in another.

One idea I used a while back I borrowed from the "Got Milk" ads. I borrowed this idea and translated it into an ad for an auto recycler. I stated boldly on the page "Got Parts! Got Guarantee! Got Fast Delivery!" Another idea I borrowed was from a flu medicine ad I found in a sports magazine. The flu ad was designed to be a consumer warning. In big letters at the top of the ad it said, "Flu Alert!" It had four strongly worded facts listed under the headline about the need to be ready for the approaching flu season. It concluded with some compelling reasons to use only their brand of flu medicine. At the top of my ad I used the headline, "Parts Alert!" Like the flu ad, I listed four strongly worded facts below the headline about recycled parts. I concluded with a list of compelling reasons to buy from my client's company.

Newspapers

Newspapers are chock full of ads, both good and bad. I think the best ones look like articles. People like to read articles and will read ads that mimic them. Even though newspaper and magazine publishers put the word "advertisement" at the top, studies show that it doesn't diminish the effectiveness of the ad.

Television

TV commercials use all kinds of dynamics to get your attention. They use testimonials, trends, humor, and even shocking statements to get your attention. The Geico Insurance ads are great direct response ads to learn from. They never seem to run out of ideas. Infomercials are another great source for ideas, especially when they get to the selling part. Notice how they give you secondary reasons to act immediately. "Ginsu Knives" with their add-on "widgets" is a great example of how to get people to place an order right away. They use the added value method to get people to respond. TV ads are also masters at using celebrity endorsements.

Radio

Radio ads, such as the Motel 6 spots featuring Matthew Odette, are good examples of effective advertising to study. Odette and Paul Harvey are masters of what is called *incident-point-benefit* ads. They tell a great story about an *incident* in order to make a *point* which dramatically illustrates a huge customer *benefit*. They are also very good at making ads that don't sound like ads.

Other sources

Always keep your eyes peeled for

ideas from anywhere you happen to be for your borrow file. You'll find them all around you. Look at ads in your social media postings, local penny shopper, on billboards, on restaurant tables and even in hotels. I found an interesting ad in my hotel room when I was at a conference. The ad was about the environment and how I could help by allowing the hotel to skip changing my sheets every day so they would save water and soap. The ad said they'd simply remake the bed for me each day. That sounded reasonable, so of course I was glad to give my permission. I took the ad with me when I left to add to my borrow file.

If you are continually on the watch for good stuff and always adding lots of ad examples to your borrow file, you will never run out of terrific ideas to make your own advertising sing!

Chapter 28
How to market your business with newsletters

A well-crafted newsletter is a way to get your foot in the door, so to speak. It helps you grab the reader's attention, engage them, and make sales. Direct mail legend, Malcom Decker, said it best, "A good company newsletter, loaded with helpful tips and interesting information, can help you nurture your customers by showing them that you care about them. It can help your customers know you, your business and your staff better. It can be a place for you to introduce new products, facility improvements, new staff and new services."

And I will add that it can be a place to sell things like recycled auto parts!

Here's how:

MAKE SALES WITH NEWSLETTERS

A well-crafted newsletter is a way to get your foot in the door, so to speak. It helps you grab the reader's attention, engage them, and make sales.

1. **Name your newsletter**. The name should reflect your newsletter's purpose and clearly give your readers an idea of what they will find inside, such as, *Johnson's Guaranteed Auto Parts & Installation Tips Monthly*.

2. **Maintain a clear customer focus**. Keep in mind the kind of customers and

prospects you are writing to and want to attract. Make your newsletter talk about the kind of things they are interested in. When writing to automotive-minded folks, for instance, be sure you are clearly "automotive" in look and in content.

3. **Create a format** and stick to it. This will keep your newsletter looking consistent from issue to issue. Decide what fonts or typestyles you will use. I suggest you use only two or three because too many will make your publication look messy and un-professional. It's usually best to stick with standard styles people are used to seeing in their local newspaper such as Times Roman typestyle for body text and Helvetica typestyle for headlines. Set your articles in two or three columns per page rather than spreading text across the entire page. Articles will look more professional and be easier to read. Dedicate certain areas of your pages for recurring features such "customer spotlight" and "upcoming events." People will come to expect these things and look for them.

4. **Tell stories**. People love to read stories. Stories can be used to solve your readers' auto parts problems. Write your stories as though you are talking to your best friend sitting across the lunch table.

5. **Include "how to" articles** and helpful tips. Remember, you are a parts expert and your newsletter should reflect your expertise. You can write about installation problems and solutions, how to get those hard to find parts, and suggest answers to the questions you get every day from customers. You can find good ideas by

subscribing to trade magazines and trade newsletters related to your customers' businesses. Be sure to get permission before reprinting anything from other publications! When you find stuff you like, write for permission to reprint them in your newsletter. Tell them you send your newsletter free to your customer mailing list. This will make a difference in how they consider your request. Most are glad to give you permission to reprint their articles as long as you don't charge your customers for it and you give proper credit.

6. **Include contact information**. Make your contact information easy to find at a glance. Readers should be able to easily find the name of your company, the name of the person to speak to, your phone number, fax number, email address and website. Don't make them look for it. Some newsletters include all this information in a small box on page one.

7. **Using photos** in your newsletter is probably the best way to draw in readers and make your newsletter look visually interesting. The right kind of photos can make your newsletter personal. Be sure to use photos wherever possible, include some of you and your staff at work and at play.

8. **Use humor and other good fillers**. Include jokes, cartoons, and other interesting fillers to make reading your newsletter fun. Obtain material from legitimate sources. Never take it without permission! Huge fines have been levied on offenders for using copyrighted cartoons without permission. But the good news is that there is a ton of copyright free mate-

INCLUDE CONTACT INFORMATION

Make your contact information easy to find at a glance. Readers should be able to easily find the name of your company, the name of the person to speak to, your phone number, fax number, email address and website.

rial available to use. You can find lots of resources by looking online. By the way, keep it decent and clean or you will lose customers and readers.

9. **Promote your products and services**. Don't forget that you are in the business of selling auto parts! Scatter small display ads or sales blurbs throughout your publication. Feature things you have to sell. Another idea is to dedicate a section or page within your newsletter for the purpose of selling. Tell readers what's new, what's on sale and/or a list of new arrivals.

10. **Consider selling ad space**. This could help you pay for your newsletter. In fact, I know of one person who sells so much space in his publication that his advertising costs are totally paid for with money left over. You can do the same by designing your newsletter to include space for other non-competitor businesses to advertise their products and services, too. If you are like most auto recyclers, your mailing list consists of a large group of auto body and general auto repair shops. There are many businesses marketing to the exact same group as you who would love to get their stuff in front of customers and prospects. Some examples of non-competitors who are marketing to the same group as you, are: machine shops, automotive electric services, equipment supply houses, muffler shops, wheel alignment/axle frame repair shops, just to name a few. You probably already know a few of them well enough to pick up the phone and ask them to be involved in your next project. It could be a win-win arrangement for both

of you!

11. **Promote upcoming issues** by including a "Coming Next Issue" blurb to let your readers know what they will find in the upcoming issue. Another idea is to have a contest or quiz with "answers next issue", so folks are looking forward to your next newsletter.

Publishing a company newsletter can serve many purposes – including, getting your name and business in front of potential customers and enhancing your image with current customers.

Chapter 29
How to green market your business

It seems like everyone wants to be green and wants to support companies that are green. This is happening because of the huge media love-fest around environmental issues. Even the current political administration (at the time of this writing) has made it a significant focus, putting money and legislation in place to further the movement.

The entertainment industry has taken up the green cause with a vengeance. They are making movies about it, incorporating it as a story line in numerous mainstream TV shows, and making it a topic on talk shows. A good example was Oprah's "Go Green Show," which was coupled with a list of "Go Green" products to buy on her website..

And who can forget the commercials starring Kermit the Frog, selling hybrid vehicles while singing, "It isn't easy being green?"

The entire green theme is showing up everywhere – in magazines, billboards, and news features. I picked up my local newspaper yesterday, and there was an article about a local grocery store who had installed a free battery charging station for customers who drive electric vehicles. "It's our way of helping the planet," they said. Of course, it is good for their business, especially after the free plug they got in the newspaper.

- Not only is it popular and politically correct to be green, it is arguably good for business. Companies everywhere are scrambling to figure out ways to make their companies and products green. There needs to be some caution, however, because of the legal implications of marketing claims. Misleading or overstating claims can lead to regulatory/civil challenges. The U.S. Federal Trade Commission provides some guidance on environmental marketing claims. Visit www.ftc.gov/bcp/grnrule/guides980427.htm for help.

IMAGE MATCH

Make sure your image matches what you're selling!

As everyone else is trying to figure out ways to *be* green, recyclers already have the advantage. They *are* green and were green before it became popular.

Here are several ways to market your green company.

Greening Your Company Image

First, you should make sure your image matches what you're selling. Yes, it's true that you are green already because you are recycling vehicles and helping the planet; but do you *look* and *act* the part in everything else you do? When people visit your facility, does it look green? Do you use recycled products? Do you recycle your paper supplies and cardboard? Do you use environmentally-friendly products everywhere you can, even in your bathrooms? Remember, perception is reality. Take a fresh look at every aspect of your business and make sure you are green in every way possible. Many green ideas can be found online with a *Google* search, as well as in books and magazines.

Educate Your Marketplace

Make it your goal to educate your own marketplace about the recycled parts industry and its commitment to the environment. It will be good for the industry, and of course, it will be good for your business. Every recycler needs to take up the cause and get the message out.

You can do this by including "green facts" in all your regular advertising. For instance, if you have a Yellow Page ad, just include a green fact or two. For instance, "Did you know that automotive recyclers recycle over 10 million vehicles each year? In doing so, they keep 11 million tons of steel and 800,000 tons of non-ferrous metals (aluminum, copper, zinc, and lead) out of landfills. Using recycled parts is good for the planet" There are plenty of green facts available for you to quote. You can find a list of them on the Automotive Recycler's Association's website, www.a-r-a.org. Also, you should send news releases whenever you do anything "green" such as making

EDUCATE ABOUT COMMITMENT TO ENVIRONMENT

Make it your goal to educate your own marketplace about the recycled parts industry and its commitment to the environment. It will be good for the industry, and of course, it will be good for your business.

175

environmentally-friendly improvements to your facility (see next chapter). Be sure to send this news release to your local newspapers and news stations along with photos. Always state in every news release your commitment to the environment.

Help Your Customers "Go Green"

Your customers, like most business owners, are feeling the pressure to go green, and you can help them. Let them know they can go green by simply adding recycled parts to the way they do business. Then they can make the same green claims you make to their customers because they are using recycled parts. Provide them with the green facts list from ARA's website and, as an example, show them how you use them in your advertising. It truly is a win-win situation for both of you!

Use Greener Methods of Advertising

There are many marketing methods that use fewer natural resources and are considered green; electronic methods such as e-mail broadcasting, website, eBay, Craig's List, Facebook, and Twitter are just a few. When you use printed items, ask for recycled paper and soy inks. If you distribute promotional products, make sure the items are environmentally friendly.

Advertise Using Green Themes

Occasionally throughout the year, create advertising for your company using green themes; green colors, and

HELP YOUR CUSTOMERS GO GREEN

Your customers, like most business owners, are feeling the pressure to go green, and you can help them. Let them know that they can go green by simply adding recycled parts to the way they do business.

graphics depicting the environment. Use powerful green headlines and subheads such as: "Save the GREEN while you save some GREEN" Use Recycled Parts, Save Money and Save the Planet? You help the environment by using recycled OEM auto parts? You save 40% to 60% cash off the cost of buying new."

Now is a great opportunity for marketing your undeniably green automotive recycling business. Automotive recyclers have a green story to tell that is authentic and genuine. Make sure you tell yours!

TELL YOUR GREEN STORY

Automotive recyclers have a green story to tell that is authentic and genuine. So make sure you tell yours!

Chapter 30
You must control your green image!

In preparation for a seminar I was giving to auto recyclers, I took a cameraman with me to the streets of my town to ask people what they honestly thought about automotive salvage yards.

One question I asked was, "Do you think an automotive salvage yard is a green business?"

Most folks said they didn't know. A few said, "Probably because they do sell parts off cars." But a surprising number of people said they thought automotive salvage yards were definitely NOT green. Some even bristled at the question and said they thought auto salvage yards are an example of the opposite of green. One lady even said the thought of junk yards made her angry because she pictured "huge piles of wrecked, rusting, chemical-oozing cars, dissolving into the earth and polluting the planet!"

I was really shocked by people in my own community responding this way! We have one automotive salvage yard in our county and it is nothing like what this last person described. I have visited that business many times and the owner is environmentally conscious. He runs a clean, earth-friendly operation. As soon as a vehicle arrives at his facility, the fluids are removed and recycled. No chemicals ever touch the ground! Parts on each vehicle are removed, placed on racks and inventoried. There are no "piles of rusting vehicles" anywhere. Vehicle hulks are kept on site for a limited time, then crushed and removed. This business has carefully met all environmental requirements and is truly green!

So, if the only automotive salvage yard in my community is so green, why do people here have such a wrong perception of it? People are probably ignorant about this business because they have never visited it. They have never seen anything positive in the local media about it. They have formed their opinion about all automotive salvage yards on information they've gotten elsewhere - most likely from TV shows and movies where salvage yards are portrayed as being junk yards full of hazardous waste.

Every auto recycler MUST work to educate their own community about their business and the industry as a whole. Here are a few suggestions:

Get your business Gold Seal Certified

The Automotive Recyclers Association (ARA) will certify you and this will give

GREEN-UP YOUR BUSINESS

Add green logos and symbols to your signs and buildings as an inexpensive way to "green-up" your business and send a positive message about what you do.

your business credibility as you achieve the highest standards within the industry. Join your state association and meet any state requirements.

Be green and clean in everything you do

Most people I interviewed told me they judged a company's greenness primarily by whether they recycled paper and plastic, used eco-friendly products within their business and used energy wisely.

Create Green Curb Appeal

People form opinions about your company by what they see when they drive by or visit. Make sure you look clean and green. A typical salvage building looks basic and ordinary but doesn't send a positive message about what goes on there. You can do an appearance survey of your facility by checking for rust damage in the front or grass growing in the pavement. Are there other signs of neglected maintenance such as faded striping on the pavement? These little maintenance problems occur slowly over time and go unnoticed by owners. Do a walk-through survey with a couple of perceptive people who are not familiar with your business. Give them a pen and paper and ask them to write down what they see that should be fixed or improved. They will notice things you don't see. Then fix those things so your facility sends a more positive message!

Paint the building!

CLEAN AND GREEN IMAGE

People form opinions about your company by what they see when they drive by or visit. Make sure you look clean and green.

This can make the most impact with the least amount of cost.

Use the word "Recycled" everywhere you can

Many within the industry are still using words like "used" or "salvage" to describe their parts. Change the word "used" to "recycled" on your sign and tell people "recycled parts are sold here". It's a first step in getting people to think of you as a recycling operation.

Add Green Logos and Symbols

Add them to your signs and buildings as an inexpensive way to "green up" your business and send a positive message about what you do.

Add a green slogan on your building

Put your slogan under your company name to tell people something positive about your business. You can use something: "Saving the planet, one part at a time", or "We were green before it was popular", or "We're extreme when it comes to being clean and green."

Put a sign near your entrance to tell your green story

This is an easy way to establish your business as green. Every business has two stories to tell; their own story of what they are doing to be green, and the recycling industry's story. Tell both. For instance, the following quote is from the United Recyclers Group:

The size of the American automotive fleet currently numbers some 270 million vehicles, nearly one apiece for every man woman and child in the country. Of these, it is estimated that nearly 11 million vehicles are taken off the road each year when they reach their so called 'End of Life' (EOL). For a typical EOL vehicle, about 75% of the parts are salvaged for reuse, about 20% of the vehicle is recycled, and the remaining 5% is thrown away. This makes an EOL vehicle one of the greenest products on the planet.

Add green landscaping & plants.

Plants bring life to any facility. But take care of them! There is nothing worse than poorly maintained plantings. There is probably someone in your company who has a love for plants. Put them in charge of keeping your plantings healthy and weeded.

Have an open house occasionally to welcome the public to your facility.

Give them a tour. This could be in conjunction with an event such as Earth Day. Invite the people in your community to be your guests. Send out news releases before and after the event to the local media.

Remember, nobody cares more about your business than you. Don't leave your image up to others. They may get it wrong.

Chapter 31

How to dramatically reduce product returns and refunds

Returned merchandise and refund requests cost your company time, effort, and money. Most companies encounter this problem to some degree, but few companies handle this situation well. They may accept refunds and returned merchandise as a normal part of doing business and act as though there is nothing they can do about it. They are WRONG.

At a recycling conference, I was sitting across the table from a couple of counter salesmen. They were from two different yards and were comparing notes about their jobs. They came to the subject of product returns. One guy got lots of them while the other guy got hardly any. They were puzzled about this. Both companies seemed to have similar products, services, and business policies. There didn't seem to be any reason for the product return difference. But one salesman experienced the problem big-time while the other one didn't.

After listening to them for a while, I discovered a major difference between the two. I noticed the salesman with many product returns was abrupt and negative to the point of rudeness. He didn't seem to like his job or his customers. A couple of times he referred to his customers as idiots. It made me wonder how he ever got a sales job. I certainly wouldn't want him speaking with any of my customers.

The guy with few returns was friendly, polite and positive. He sounded like he genuinely liked and respected his customers. He said how good it felt to solve a customer's problem. You could tell that he received much personal satisfaction from making his customers happy. I knew I had the answer to the product return mystery. A salesman's attitude about his job and customers makes a big difference in product returns! This is a good argument for employers monitoring phone calls so they can know how sales-staff speak to customers.

A salesman's attitude is only part of reason for product returns. Let's look at some other possibilities:

Faulty or Damaged Merchandise. This problem can be reduced or eliminated with proper quality control systems in place. Begin by getting your business CAR Certified. You can do this by calling ARA, (703) 385-1001.

Poor Service. This is a fixable problem. You can bring in professionals to train your staff.

Dishonest Customers. Any business will occasionally encounter someone who wants to get something for nothing and doesn't intend to pay. Fortunately, most customers are satisfied with honest value for their money. You can refuse to do business with bad customers to eliminate the problem of dealing with them.

Better Price Somewhere Else. While price can be a factor, it's rarely the reason a customer will give for a refund or return decision.

Buyer's Remorse. This reason is different than the first four listed above. It is a tougher problem with a far more difficult solution because it is emotional in nature. No amount of practical, logical problem solving is going to be completely effective in combating it. But, something can be done. Read on.

How to Put an Abrupt End to Buyer's Remorse

Because buyer's remorse is emotional in nature you must have an emotional answer for the problem. A big part of the solution is in knowing when buyer's remorse begins. It strikes your customer the moment the purchase is made. As soon as your customer has made a big purchase from you something like this starts to go on in his mind:

"Maybe I made a mistake. I should have shopped around for a better price. I bet I could have gotten it cheaper if I had looked a little harder."

"I must be an idiot for spending so much money on this. My wife (boss, friends, co-workers) are going to think I'm nuts for getting this. There's no way this thing will

DEAL EFFECTIVELY WITH BUYER'S REMORSE

Learn to see things from your customer's perspective; this will enable you to put an abrupt end to the big problem of buyer's remorse (a big reason for many returns), and help you to give them needed post-purchase reassurance, that they have made a wise and excellent purchase!

work for what I need it for. Something will probably go wrong with it."

"I should take this thing back and get my money back. If they won't give me my money back, I'll sue them."

According to marketers who've studied this behavior, this is known as the "buyer's remorse chorus." This chorus starts the moment a big purchase is made. That's when you must begin to deal with it.

Most business owners think they are an exception to this problem. They think buyer's remorse won't happen to their customers. They're wrong! This problem effects every business and service in some way. Those who fail to recognize the problem and deal with it are losing more than they realize. Business owners deny this problem because they see their business through their own eyes and not through the eyes of their customers. The truth is, nearly every business owner believes his or her business is the finest of its kind. They make the fatal error of assuming that their customers feel the same way. But customers don't. A customer thinks about himself and what he's going to get. It's a natural human tendency. When you were a child at a party and the mom served cake and ice cream, the kids would jump up and say, "me first, me first!" Now you're an adult, when refreshments are served, you don't jump up and say "me first, me first!" - but you still THINK it!

To deal with the "buyer's remorse

chorus" you must learn to see things from your customer's perspective. This will enable you to put an abrupt end to the "buyers remorse chorus".

By the way, another reason business owners are unaware of the "buyer's remorse" problem is because most customers returning items because of buyer's remorse actually give phony reasons for the return instead of just admitting they had second thoughts about their purchase.

Remember our two counter salesmen at the beginning of this story? One got many returns and the other rarely got any. The one with few returns did something extra with every sale. This extra ingredient, added to each sale, made it difficult for his customers to experience buyer's remorse. He gave them Post-Purchase Reassurance! That is: he reassured his customers that the purchase they made from him was a wise one. He reassured them that they had gotten what they wanted and their worries were unfounded. Post-purchase reassurance assures a customer that the choice they made was a good one and removes doubts about how people will view them or judge them. It turns off the "buyer's remorse chorus". What they heard instead at the end of the sale were statements like, "This is a great front-end you just bought! It is an excellent purchase. You're getting it at a fantastic bargain, too! You're saving half off list price! That's a lot of extra money in your pocket! I'm sure glad I was able to help you get the right clip at such fantastic savings. I know you're gonna be glad you bought it!

Another way to add post-purchase reassurance to a sale is to write a personal follow-up letter immediately after the purchase. Even though this may not be practical for small purchases, a simple thank you note will do. It is a very good idea for those big substantial purchases you want to make stick. Companies who use post-purchase reassurance letters regularly find that they reduce returns significantly. The reason is that a buying decision is primarily an emotional decision - even for the most sophisticated buyer who uses logic and intellect to rationalize and support their emotional decision. Your post-purchase reassurance letter will soothe your customer's wavering emotions. In your letter, thank them for their purchase, restate benefits of what they bought, give additional information and tips to get the most from their purchase, assure them they made a wise choice and thank them again for their purchase. Include your phone number and invite them to call you with any further questions or needs.

The only return you want to get is return business!

PERSONAL FOLLOW-UP LETTER

Another way to add post-purchase reassurance to a sale is to write a personal follow-up letter immediately after the purchase. Even though this may not be practical for small purchases, a simple thank you note will do.

Tip Index

Coupons really do make a difference in sales!

How to get lost customers back

How to get and use powerful testimonials

How to get published in the newspaper

Ethics will make or break you

Developing a borrow file for fresh ideas

How to market your business with newsletters

How to green market your business

You must control your green image!

How to dramatically reduce product returns and refunds

Everybody has a personal story to share, and I have

one too. To read mine, please visit:

www.mikefrench.com/mystory